FIVE WOMEN
of the
ENGLISH REFORMATION

FIVE WOMEN
of the
ENGLISH REFORMATION

Paul F. M. Zahl

Woodland Lutheran
Library

WILLIAM B. EERDMANS PUBLISHING COMPANY
GRAND RAPIDS, MICHIGAN / CAMBRIDGE, U.K.

© 2001 Wm. B. Eerdmans Publishing Co.
All rights reserved

Wm. B. Eerdmans Publishing Co.
255 Jefferson Ave. S.E., Grand Rapids, Michigan 49503 /
P.O. Box 163, Cambridge CB3 9PU U.K.

06 05 04 03 02 01   7 6 5 4 3 2

Library of Congress Cataloging-in-Publication Data

Zahl, Paul F. M.
Five women of the English Reformation / Paul F. M. Zahl.
p.   cm.
Includes bibliographical references.
ISBN 0-8028-3825-1 (CLOTH : ALK. PAPER)
1. REFORMATION — England. 2. Women — Biography.
I. Title.
BR375 .Z34 2001
274.2'06'0922 — dc21
[B]

2001040275

www.eerdmans.com

*This book is dedicated to
Robin Anderson, Lynn Adams, Mary Zahl, and Fran Cade,
Birmingham women of the Reformation.*

Contents

Contents

Introduction

High-born intellectual women played a leading role in the Protestant Reformation. Among the more prominent were Marguerite de Navarre, Renée de France, and Jeanne d'Albret in France; Argula von Grumbach, Katharina of Mecklenburg, Ursula Riedinger, and Katharina von Bora in Germany; and, in England, Anne Boleyn, Anne Askew, Katharine Parr, Jane Grey, Catherine Willoughby, and finally, Elizabeth Tudor.

This book is a short study of this last group of six women of the English Reformation. Among these women were queens regent, instructors to kings, and powerful symbolic figureheads. All were extremely well educated by the standards of their time. They were also sincere in the Reformed Religion to the point of actual martyrdom: two were beheaded (Anne Boleyn and Jane Grey), one was tortured and burned at the stake (Anne Askew), one was forced into exile (Catherine Willoughby), one was imprisoned (Elizabeth Tudor), and one *almost* lost her head (Katharine Parr). The book concludes with a note on Anne Bradstreet, who was a child on Catherine Willoughby's former estates at Tattershall before coming with the Puritans to America.

Most of these women have been studied and are well known to historians. Only Anne Boleyn and her daughter Elizabeth will be well known to the common reader. One aspect, however, which singularly and decisively united all of them, is *not* well known. It is the most important single fact about them. It is that aspect which each of them said was the most important characteristic of their lives. This was their highly focused, indeed intense by any standard, interest in the Christian religion. Our subjects were absolutely and unconditionally committed to the advance of true Christianity as they understood it. They were each one of them extremely — one could almost say muscularly and monocularly — focused on the *theological* concerns of their day.

Anne Boleyn left behind a revealing theological library. Anne Askew debated her way through the eucharistic question right through to its being the ostensible reason for her own death. It was a death that her incisive, systematic theology made inevitable. Katharine Parr wrote a devotional book entitled *Lamentation of a Sinner.* When she was fourteen years old, Jane Grey wrote letters in Latin to the Zürich Reformer Heinrich Bullinger. She received studious replies. Jane Grey, "Queen Jane" for nine days, fought off life-and-death efforts to convert her to Rome when she was only sixteen! She resisted those efforts with reason, even erudition, and watertight argument against a doctor in theology twice her age. Catherine Willoughby protected the preacher-bishop Hugh Latimer until things became so hot for her under Mary Tudor that she had to flee for her life to the Netherlands, a nursing baby at her breast. Elizabeth Tudor, who had learned very young to be circumspect in matters of theology, nevertheless translated a French Protestant devotional book into English. The women I speak of were all theologians. It is the theological aspect of their remarkable achievement as human beings and as women which this book seeks to underline.

Introduction

MANY aspects of life were common to all of these women: high social class and standing; the uncommonly good education almost all of them received; more leisure than women of other inherited stations of life; even their relations with men, which make interesting reading. None of these common facts, however, was the decisive thing *so far as the women themselves saw things*. We require a "paradigm shift" away from external circumstances if we are to appreciate these women as they understood themselves.

We could say that as women born to aristocracy and even monarchy, they, unlike other women of their period, were empowered by accident of birth to *do* something. It is certainly true that their education was a product solely of their rank. It was a Renaissance ideal for many highborn women to receive a classical education, in particular to study Latin and Greek, as well as French. It was widely reported of Lady Jane Grey that she was "caught" at age twelve reading Plato's *Phaedo* in Greek.

On the other hand, many equally highborn ladies were less interested in theology than these women were, and passed their time doing the endless needlepoint to which aristocratic women were condemned in the sixteenth century. Noble women, in other words, did not all spend their leisure time reading books in ancient languages. A woman's social class was no guarantee of a theological inclination. Power and noble birth are not sufficient to account for these women's assertive and determined cut-and-thrust Christian ideals.

We could focus instead on gender both in describing and in interpreting the careers of these women. Certainly gender affected the conflicts which bruised each one of them so. Anne Boleyn derived her influence, or, better, her political clout, entirely from her relationship with King Henry, but then her tragic end derived from him also. Anne Askew liked at times to disparage herself, with irony, as a "poor" and "ignorant" female, which helped her out of some tight spots during her early interrogations. But being a divorced woman made her more vulnerable to those interrogations in the first place. Katharine Parr died in childbirth during her fourth, star-struck marriage to Thomas Seymour, who was regarded by his contemporaries as a seducer and superficial person. Jane Grey was forced absolutely against her will into an arranged marriage with Guilford Dudley. It was that marriage which set up the chain of events that led directly to Jane's catastrophic nine-days reign in 1553. Catherine Willoughby was first married at age thirteen, to a man thirty-five years her elder. Finally, Elizabeth Tudor, by remaining single, avoided such entanglements as had proven disastrous, in one form or another, for all her high-profile female predecessors in the Reformed Religion.

On the other hand, Boleyn, Askew, Parr, Grey, and Willoughby were all heterosexual women who never would have questioned the norm of marriage in principle. Marriage was expected by them as well as of them. Boleyn, Parr, and Willoughby were happily married, by the plain testimony of their written remains and recorded conversations, or at least were happily married for certain periods. If we were able to ask them whether gender played a role in their theological activity — which was their main conscious focus — they would not, with the possible exception of Anne Askew, know what we were talking about. And if they did understand what we were talking about, if they were given to hear of the idea that gender is a constitutive element of the human being, each would reject it absolutely without any question as an element in their theological thinking.

The paradigm of gender does not explain the content of these women's work. It is true they all developed an explicit allergy to what they understood to be "superstition," i.e., transubstantiation and the mass. While their allergy to superstition, expressed ironically and with some humor, might be seen as opposition to male authority, as represented by the church, their main principles of theology were shared point for point with many men who worked alongside them. They were part of a religious movement which transcended gender. They knew this, and said it. Cranmer knew it, and said it. As did Latimer; as did Matthew Parker, who loved Anne Boleyn and became Archbishop of Canterbury under her daughter; as did John Bale, Anne Askew's advocate, editor, and posthumous publisher; as did Lord Burleigh, Catherine Willoughby's support; as did Guilford Dudley, Jane's reluctant husband who later died with her. As did even Jane's truculent, finally courageous father. These men all shared the views of the women with whose lives they were bound.

All of these women thought theologically. They were lay theologians. They read theological books, most especially the Bible, and anything to which they could gain access from the continental Protestant Reformers. They talked theology. Their inner circles of court ladies were twenty-four-hours-a-day Bible studies. They saw everything that happened to them through two lenses: the lens of the providence of God and the lens of the furtherance of the Reformed Religion. They pressed their case with patience, perseverance, and courage. They sometimes pressed their case unwisely. The cause that mattered to them was, in their language, the simple Gospel of Christ as given in the Scriptures. Each of these women, even and especially Anne Boleyn, King Henry's willing wife, lived for one thing: to see the Reformed Religion overcome the opposition to it both within the church and outside it. They ached to see the Reformation triumph. They were not only observers of this high drama, they were participants. They saw themselves that way.

I myself am a systematic theologian by training and a parish minister by profession. I am neither a professional historian nor an academic teacher. But a theologian working in parish ministry can aspire to insight regarding these women of the English Reformation. Why? Because I believe I understand these women *from the inside out.* When I read their work, I believe what they were saying. When I study their answers to hostile questions in the context of interrogation and under the threat of torture, I wonder if I would answer under pressure as they answered. A Christian of any time and place will find herself or himself to be a soul mate with each of these women within the impasses in which they found themselves. Could I keep my head, figuratively and also literally? Would I stand true to that on which I have placed my own life's hopes? Would I be able to put God and Bible first, my own person second? For Christian people, it is a straightforward exercise to live with these women from the inside out.

THERE are two sources of evidence on these leading women of the English Reformation that provide a window into their thoughts and self-understanding: their writings and letters, and their recorded conversations.

All of them but Anne left behind considerable if somewhat occasional written work. It is extraordinary that Katharine Parr produced a book. It is in a definite genre and thus quite derivative of similar works produced before it in France. But it *is* a book and is in her hand, every word of it. In addition, their letters were valued by the receivers, especially in hindsight. Thus we know what we know about Catherine Willoughby because some of her sharp, unguarded letters have survived, along with a few pathetic letters from her old age. The appendices below feature written remains of these five Reformation women.

Because each of them was in the public eye to a lesser or greater degree, their words and actions were often recorded, sometimes in word-for-word detail. Like Bishops Cranmer, Ridley, Latimer, and Hooper, their words under interrogation were recorded with legal precision. Thus Askew and Grey were able to give unmistakable voice to their systematic, thought-through interpretations of Scripture.

The stories of these five women, who were nursing mothers of the English Reformation, are text-anchored because texts exist, except for Anne Boleyn, for whom we have only Thomas Cranmer's letter to King Henry pleading for mercy on Anne's behalf. This letter is important not only for what it communicates about Anne's theological perspective, but also for what it says about her value in the eyes of her fellow Reformers.

Two issues need to be settled at the start. First, why is Elizabeth Tudor (1533-1603) not given her own chapter? In one sense, Elizabeth is very much included, for the success of the Protestant cause during and as a result of her reign was the climax, even the summary, of what her five younger "sisters" sought so passionately to achieve in their brief time of influence. Elizabeth I is the capstone of a pyramid comprised of at least these five martyred and ill-used lesser lights — lesser lights, that is, in terms of the world. Elizabeth even shared their sufferings in that she was imprisoned for eighteen months under her half-sister, Queen Mary. Elizabeth was a Protestant in her genes, because her mother was Anne Boleyn and her legitimacy was denied formally and forever by the Church of Rome. She was a Protestant, in other words, by compulsion, as Rome would never recognize her status as queen of England. Elizabeth was also, at least to some degree, a Protestant by conviction, although she was more conservative, or, rather, more cautious, than her "sisters." In addition, she was educated by Protestant tutors and taught from Protestant texts.

But Elizabeth was also her father's child. She realized that it was wise politically to play both ends against the middle. So her policy was never unambiguously Protestant. In fact, she considered Catherine Willoughby's religion, which was Puritan, distasteful and overzealous, even self-serving. Elizabeth reacted to definite Protestant principles in religion somewhat in the way "mainstream" Presbyterians say they experience the P.C.A.! Elizabeth Tudor's religion represents the triumph of the Reformation in England, but she herself stood somewhat apart from it. Her principles, whatever they were exactly, never showed upon her sleeve the way they did with Anne, Anne, Katharine, Jane, and Catherine. The Fairy Queen keeps to a different category. She will come directly into the story only with the account of Catherine Willoughby's acute and ardent dissatisfaction with the pace of reform in the 1560s. Elizabeth was a daughter, not a mother of the English Reformation.

Second, the main concern of this book is theological. It is not a biographical survey, although the basic facts are included. Instead, the focus is on the theological perspective of five sixteenth-century women regarding (1) the life of the Christian church; concerning (2) the life of the nation as they longed for it to become; and concerning (3) themselves personally, caught as they were in power struggles and conflicts that put them in the lethal sights of their enemies as soon as they had declared themselves religiously.

On the other hand, my hope is that the book goes beyond theological concerns as well. The power and appeal of these women, remarkable by any standard, makes them rich subjects for reflection and emulation. The personalities of these five women, women who spoke their minds with presence of mind and sharp intelligence within situations of life-and-death duress, are almost totemic in our enduring search for role models.

I, for one, was captivated in my thirties by the 1985 film of Jane Grey's struggle entitled *Lady Jane*. This film, directed by Trevor Nunn and written by David Edgar, made an impressive effort to be accurate. My own identification with Jane, a child-adult of 16, revealed something important to me concerning my own most personal commitments both as a theologian and as a human being.

Katharine Parr, too, can carry you away with her selfless yet thoroughly human, even vulnerable, approach to Christianity. Anne Askew is a harder character to love, as she was tart, ironic, and also iron. Anne Boleyn is difficult to get hold of, for there is less evidence and she died so suddenly! Catherine Willoughby, while endearing in her early adulthood and stoic in the sudden and over-whelming loss of her two young sons, simply lived too long! She ended her life isolated and cantankerous, presiding over an exhausting agricultural estate in Lincolnshire under a queen whose caution and withholding had embittered her.

The point is, these are accessible, real human beings, not cut off from us by the passage of many years. To read their legacy is to read the familiar. The saying that "the past is different, they do things differently there" is simply not true. *Human nature is evenly distributed* and through all time and place. That maxim is made evident in the lives of five young, focused, and well-attested women from the middle decades of the sixteenth century. Life and theology intersect, even in this mainly theological study.

I would like to thank my wife, Mary, who provides an important epilogue, a contemporary woman's perspective. Mark Lester of Birmingham-Southern College read the manuscript and gave important input. I wish also to thank Nita Moorhead, who has worked tirelessly and selflessly in the production of this book.

Chapter One

ANNE BOLEYN

(1507-1536)

PROLOGUE

The Protestant Reformation in England was a movement to re-
store the Christian religion in that country to the original values of
Christianity as described in the New Testament. This Reformation
took 168 years to achieve success, beginning with the entry into England around 1520 of the insights of Martin Luther and concluding
with the constitutional establishment of Protestantism at the time
of the Glorious Revolution of 1688. With the exile of King James II,
a Roman Catholic, and the accession of William of Orange, a
Protestant, England became explicitly, across almost all classes of
people and interest groups, a country that understood itself as
Protestant rather than as Catholic. This is undeniable fact. Every
attempt that has ever been made to deny that England by the late
1600s was the leading Protestant nation in Europe has always had
to plead, "Don't confuse me with the facts." England was an over-
whelmingly Protestant country until recently, and now it is simply
searching for faith in something rather than *non-Protestant* in any sense
of that expression.

There was a breathless and seemingly unending number of false starts, reversals, and "new" beginnings from 1520 to 1688, such that at several moments of crisis it was anyone's guess what the final result would be. England passed through more than one period of apparent re-catholicization before the issue was settled. Even the Oxford or Tractarian Movement of the nineteenth century was an intellectual and aesthetic attempt to reverse the Reformation.

But the fundamental common self-understanding was from 1688 and forever after Protestant. To read the Sovereign's Coronation Oath, as it was administered from the early 1700s and still read at coronations through the nineteenth century, is to be confronted with the decisive finality of the Reformation's success in England. It is important to print the Oath here. It settles the question of whether official English Christianity is Catholic or Protestant.

I, ———, do solemnly and sincerely, in the presence of God, profess, testify, and declare that I do believe that in the sacrament of the Lord's Supper there is not any transubstantiation of the elements of bread and wine into the body and blood of Christ, at or after the consecration thereof, by any person whatsoever; and that the invocation or adoration of the Virgin Mary or any other Saint, and the sacrifice of the mass, as they are now used in the Church of Rome, are superstitious, and idolatrous. And I do solemnly, in the presence of God, profess, testify, and declare, that I do make this declaration, and every part thereof, in the plain and ordinary sense of the words read unto me, as they are commonly understood by English Protestants, without any evasion, equivocation, or mental reservation, and without any dispensation already granted me for this purpose by the Pope or any other authority or person whatsoever, or without any hope of any such dispensation from any person or authority whatsoever, or without thinking that I am or can be acquitted before God or man, or absolved of this declaration or any part thereof, although the Pope, or any other person or persons or power whatsoever, shall dispense with or annul the same, or declare that it was null and void from the beginning.

The five women portrayed in this book devoted the core energies of their lives to contending for the ideas expressed in that oath.

THERE is a further important point of prologue to make before Anne Boleyn enters the stage. Why did medieval Roman Catholicism engender the hurricane of absolutely and unconditionally negative reaction represented by these women of the English Reformation? What was it in the Catholic understanding of Christ and church which created such massive focused criticism?

There are at least two reasons for the Reformation protest against Roman Catholicism. They are bound together. First, Catholicism sought to objectify, or make concrete and palpable, the relation between God and humanity. *This cannot be done.* The relation between God and humanity is, like all relationships in life, unseen. Love is unseen. Forgiveness and affection, malice and animus: relationships exist within the invisible theater of emotions and feelings. People who are emotionally hungry know this. You cannot buy off with things someone who hates you, except maybe for five minutes. Nor can you get someone to love you by means of gifts, that is, at least, until the heart loves. Jane Austen taught this in *Pride and Prejudice.* Lord Darcy is unable to win Elizabeth Bennet's affection, absolutely and paralyzingly unable to win her heart, until his personal sacrifice and selflessness win it. His grand houses and estate, his reputation, his connections: nothing of his that is exterior to himself is sufficient to win the love of his life. It is a maxim that love is totally powerful and also totally invisible.

Our Reformation women knew that.

These women could not possibly endure a system of "meritorious" actions and offerings and indulgences and pilgrimages and prostrations that did not reflect the authentic *inwardness* of life and love. So they rejected, absolutely forcefully, the characteristic attempts of Roman Catholicism to objectify or make tangible that which is subjective and intangible.

Second, as a result of their insight regarding the primacy of the inward, Anne Boleyn, Anne Askew, Katharine Parr, Jane Grey, and Catherine Willoughby all developed an allergy to superstition. Superstition is the idea that a concrete object handled in a definite way possesses power, negative or positive. Superstition attaches invisible hopes to visible things. Reality, however, scuttles superstition.

Reformation women observed the fallacy of superstition and challenged it. They challenged it tenaciously and unremittingly.

Thus medieval Catholicism, with its attempts to objectify God and God's relation to us, strengthened by a regressive human tendency to crave such objectivity and bring our own superstition to the equation, had to come down! The church had to come down — at least in the face of our Reforming women's X-ray vision. They pierced the veil of human cravenness and puerility, and pierced in doing so the age-old veil of the Temple (St. Matthew 27:51).

ANNE BOLEYN'S LIFE IN BRIEF

Anne Boleyn, the bane of that virtuous and religious Queen Katherine, the ruin of many pious, worthy and famous men who favored not that unlawful marriage, the first giver of entrance to the Protestant religion. . . .[1]

---

1. From the papers of the family of Sir Thomas Tresham of Rushton, whose intense Roman Catholicism is preserved in stone in the ruins of Lyveden New Bield

*What a zealous defender she was of Christ's gospel all the world
doth know, and her acts do and will declare to the world's end.*[2]

Anne Boleyn was twenty-six years old when she became Queen of
England. She was twenty-nine when she was executed for treason
against the King.

Anne was born in Norfolk to a family that we would describe
today as *nouveau riche* and ambitious. Anne's father and her brother,
together with Anne herself, worked single-mindedly for the ad-
vancement of their family's interests at the court of Henry VIII.
What distinguished them from other courtiers, however, was their
early acceptance of the New Religion, as it was called at first: the
Protestant insight regarding the message of the New Testament as
it emanated from Germany after 1517. George Boleyn, Lord Rochford, Anne's brother, became an extremely committed and articulate advocate of Protestant Reform in England. Anne shared his
views precisely, probably even more deeply,[3] and almost definitely
with more learning.

Anne was educated in France from the age of six. Her seven
years in the royal courts of Burgundy, Flanders, Amboise (and
Cloux, where Leonardo da Vinci served the French king), and Paris
gave her a delight in the French language; an extremely cosmopoli-
tan exposure to Renaissance classicism and also fashion — for it is
proven beyond a doubt that she forever after loved fine clothes and

---

and at Kettering's Triangular Lodge (right along the modern railway line), both in
Northamptonshire. The quotation is taken from E. W. Ives, *Anne Boleyn* (Oxford: Oxford University Press, 1986), 60.

2. From John Foxe's *Acts and Monuments* (1837-41 edition), vol. 5, p. 175, as quoted
in Ives, *Anne Boleyn*, 302.

3. Lord Rochford's address on the scaffold just before his execution could be
read as containing a percentage of recantation. Not so Anne's! In a parallel case, the
scaffold address by Lady Jane Grey's father, Henry Grey, is just as committed and uncompromising as that of his sixteen-year-old daughter.

jewelry; and a strong, living link to a heritage she had in common with most of her sisters in the English Reformation. This heritage was the French connection, a Reforming tendency which existed at the highest level of the French nobility. This Reforming fervor was embodied in Marguerite of Angoulême (later known as the Queen of Navarre), Gillaume de Briçonnet, her Reformist bishop, and Jacques Lefèvre d'Étaples, the humanist Bible translator and influential polymath. "Lutheran" ideas, as all the insights of the Reformed Religion were at first labeled by their opponents, came to France through these three brilliant individuals. It is through their writings, specifically, that the Reformation insight first came to Anne Boleyn.

The Reformation insight, which was justification by grace through faith and the consequent disenchantment with the Catholic church, was to come to Anne, and thus to Queen Anne, from a French Bible, from French commentaries on Scripture, and from the anti-establishment, Reformist poetry of Clément Marot. The French connection was not unmediated, insofar as Anne never knew Marguerite de Navarre *as* Reformer, nor was she old enough to comprehend the issues involved during the period she lived in France as a very young child. But Anne's delight in the French language made the works she began to receive as gifts later on as a young adult, entirely accessible and also pleasant to her. Anne received the Reformation, in other words, partly because she understood its third principal language, its first language being Latin and its second being Greek. English is the fourth language of Reformation literature. The earliest Reformation works in English were translations of Luther from his German and Latin.

Anne Boleyn's story intersects with that of Henry Tudor at the point that King Henry began to be impatient with the inability of his first wife, Katherine of Aragon, to produce a male heir. Although she was not regarded as a beauty by her contemporaries, Anne's inward confidence and outward vivacity caught the king's eye on hunting excursions during which her family sought to put themselves forward for royal preferment.

Around the beginning of Lent 1526, Henry began to go after Anne. The following winter he decided on a divorce from Katherine. The story of his divorce and the nation-shaking events that led to his marriage to Anne on January 24 or 25, 1533 (she had become pregnant) is well known and quite complex. Anne's coronation as Queen of England took place on Whitsunday (i.e., Pentecost), June 1, 1533.

ANNE BOLEYN was executed on Friday, April 19, 1536. The length of her reign, just under three years, has inspired the nickname, "Anne of the Thousand Days." During this period she gave birth to a daughter, Elizabeth, who was later declared a bastard both under English law — the ruling was reversed later when circumstances changed — and also under Roman Catholic church law. The second ruling was never reversed. It fortified the pope's declaration that Anne's daughter was entirely illegitimate as Queen of England and therefore the legitimate target of a *fatwah*.

During her thousand days, Anne, supported by like-minded Reformers such as Thomas Cromwell at court and Thomas Cranmer within the church, presided over the Reformation of the Church of England. Anne, leaning on Henry, fomented a policy of dissolving all the monasteries, although she also worked actively towards the use of the riches and lands thus expropriated for the relief of the poor. There is incontrovertible evidence of this. At the same time, many nobles who stood to gain from the Dissolution resented Anne's claims on expropriated property for the relief of the destitute. This resentment probably led in part to widespread support for the *coup d'état* that crushed her.

Anne also secured, again through Henry — as her good works were almost always achieved from and through her husband's authority — the appointment of several evangelical bishops and deans for the newly independent Church of England. Anne was also patron to Protestant publishers and writers, who were able to become extremely prolific during this Protestant period of royal policy. Thus Anne sought to convince Henry that William Tyndale, the outlaw Bible translator and "Lutheran" theologian, was the king's supporter and friend. That was basically true, in any event.

For reasons that have never become clear, Thomas Cromwell, who was by theological conviction and government policy a supporter of Anne's and of the Protestant party's goals at court, turned on her, with seeming suddenness, in the early months of 1536. He later told the Hapsburg ambassador to England that he, Cromwell, had engineered the coup: the false charges of adultery against Anne; the charges of collusion with her brother, Lord Rochford; the startling speed of their arrest and trial; the "evidence" presented to King Henry as well as the "witnesses"; the engineered trials — everything! Cromwell's motives have never been understood. Possibly he thought to avert Henry's suspicion of himself by setting the king on to Anne.

In any event, Anne denied all the charges at the trial, as did Rochford her brother. She carried herself with affecting poise right up to the moment of her death. At that moment she spoke earnestly, but without grievance, of the faith in which she was to die. Cranmer met with her as confessor and chaplain the day before her execution. We will never know what passed between them, although we do have Cranmer's letter to Henry, the most difficult of his career, defending Anne as best he could. He had been kept sedulously in the dark, right up to the last minute, concerning the accusations and their sources. His painful yet brilliant letter managed at the same time to defend Anne, to submit no less absolutely to the king's judgment, *and* to speak for the Reformed Religion that Anne herself had demonstratively backed.

Anne died meekly but gave away nothing. She was then completely erased from the record. It became as if she had never lived.

The value of her achievement only began to be understood after her daughter Elizabeth became queen twenty-five years later. It was then that John Foxe, the Protestant chronicler, was able to tell Anne's story, at least as he and many of her contemporaries had grasped it at the time.

WHAT sort of person was Anne? What was her inward life like? We cannot really know. We have windows into Anne Askew's spiritedness, into Katharine Parr's penitence and prescience, into Jane Grey's "back talking" in the face of danger, and into Catherine Willoughby's desperation at being excluded from court and thus from influence by Elizabeth I.

Anne Boleyn's temperament and personal qualities, on the other hand, have to be deduced from a few bits of written evidence, such as the lists of her fabulous wardrobe and the fact that she sent back one of her infant Elizabeth's caps three times to the designer at Greenwich until it was just so. We also have her unflappable, firm "No!" to every charge that was laid publicly against her at the trial.

But what was really in her mind? How did she really regard her husband? What did she say to Cranmer the day before she died — in an appointment that lasted two hours? And how did she regard herself as she laid her head on the block that Friday? There is no way to know. Of her theology, however, of her specific commitments in Christianity, we know a good deal.

THE TEXTS

Anne treasured a 1534 edition of the Bible in French, printed in Antwerp. It was the translation by Jacques Lefèvre d'Étaples. Its frontcover and back-cover inscriptions let us know immediately that it is an evangelical and therefore a Reformed book:

AINSI + QUE + TOUS + MEURENT + PAR + ADAM:
AUSSY + TOUS + SERONT + VIVIFIES + PAR + CHRIST
(*As in Adam all die, so will all be raised to life again by Christ*
[This is a summary of Romans 5:12-18].)

LA + LOY + A + ESTE + DONNE + PAR + MOYSSE:
LA + GRACE + ET + LA + VERITE + PAR + IESU
   + CHRIST.
(*For the law was given through Moses; grace and truth came
through Jesus Christ* [St. John 1:17].)

The Reformation antithesis of law and gospel is expressed epi-
grammatically through this concluding verse of the Prologue to St.
John. Having this verse embossed on the cover of the Bible was a
statement, what today is called a "signal," of the core view of the
interpreter elect, i.e., of the reader, i.e., of Anne Boleyn the elect
reader!

Anne also possessed a now incalculably precious copy of William Tyndale's 1534 edition of the New Testament. Although a
banned book, it seems to have been a presentation copy. Anne also
owned two illuminated manuscripts in French that were explicitly
Protestant in theology: the "Epistle and Gospel for the 52 Sundays
in the Year," translated from the French of Lefèvre d'Étaples again;
and a commentary on Ecclesiastes, the author of which is un-
known. She possessed as well a copy of "Le Pasteur Evangélique"
(i.e., "The Gospel Shepherd") by Clément Marot. Marot's poetry
included the Huguenot Psalter and numerous elegies to Christ.

From these books, which can still be seen today, books which
existed then on the highest possible shelf of controversy and danger, it is possible to give an account of Anne Boleyn's theology.

HER THEOLOGY

The particular kind of Reformist criticism that Anne and her court party applied to the church has much in common with the fairly widespread critique of excess and abuse for which Erasmus of Rotterdam was famous. This is to say, it was not the core of Roman Catholic faith and use that was wrong, but rather the wrong and self-serving ends to which that core had been put in service of the visible, institutional church.

At first sight, therefore, the sustained and caustic attack on church institutions that Anne supported from 1533 to 1536 looks Erasmian. Anne got the King to remove a famous relic, the "blood of Hailes," from Hailes Abbey and was therefore successful in shutting down the veneration of what was soon discovered to be duck's blood.[4] A further, memorable case of the initiative she sought to take in closing down the monasteries was her visit to Syon at the end of December 1535. Syon was a convent of the wellborn and is now regarded as a sort of early sixteenth-century equivalent of Port-Royal-les-Champs in the next century in France. It combined aristocracy, learning, and particularly intense commitment to the church's faith. Accompanied by her chaplain, William Latimer, Anne entered the church at Syon as the sixty nuns were prostrate in prayer, all their backs to her. She gave a short speech and urged En-

4. The site of Hailes Abbey in Gloucestershire is of interest to the readers of this book. Side by side with the manicured and well-marked remains of the Abbey is the parish church, one of the best-preserved, absolutely Protestant church interiors remaining in the Church of England. It is the entire Reformation condensed into one small space: a preaching church focused on the pulpit, with the chancel behind retaining its "Puritan" arrangements for Holy Communion, a table around the four sides of which the communicants knelt (or sat) at one sitting. Directly outside the church are the plinths and aisles of the shrine that was built for the duck's blood. Interestingly, visitors today are guided in such a way as to become more rhapsodic over the supposed romance of the medieval ruins than the republican statement formed by the adjoining church's brilliant interior.

glish-language primers on them to replace the Latin ones they used. She got nowhere with the sisters. It was a little embarrassing.

Such episodes as Hailes and Syon seem to link Anne with Reformist interests throughout Europe, which lampooned superstition and corruption within the church from Regensburg to Canterbury. But as always in accounts of the English Reformation, it is a dangerous error to underestimate the specifically religious theological context behind these attacks on abuse. Anne Boleyn was more than a Reformist; she was a Reformer, i.e., a partisan of the Protestant Reformation of the church's theology.

The heart of Anne's theology is plain to see in a book she treasured: the English translation of a French commentary on Ecclesiastes. Here is an excerpt from the section on Ecclesiastes 12:13 ("The end of the matter; all has been heard. Fear God, and keep his commandments; for this is the whole duty of man"). The issue for the Protestant commentator is this: which comes first in the ethical (i.e., the Christian) life, faith in Christ or works of the law? The tree or the fruit of the tree?

> For faith which giveth the true fear of God, is it that doth prepare for us for to keep the commandments well, and maketh us good workmen for to make good works, and maketh us good trees for to bear good fruit. Then if we be not first well prepared, made good workmen, and made good trees, we may not look to do the least of the commandments. Therefore Moses giving the commandments "said: 'Harken, Israel, thy God is one god, which is as much as to say as'": without faith God does not profit us, nor can we accomplish [anything]: but the faith in God, and in our Lord Jesus Christ is it which doth relieve us from the transgressions that be passed of the sentence of the law, and yieldeth us innocents, and in such manner that none can demand of us anything, for because that faith hath gotten us

21

Jesus Christ, and maketh him our own, he having accomplished the law, and satisfied unto all transgressions . . . Whereby [the Holy Ghost] engendereth in us true childerly fear, and putteth away all servile and hired fear. And then it sheddeth in our hearts the fire of love and dilection, [i.e., delight] by the means whereof we be well prepared for to keep the law of God, which is but love. . . . For our hearts [without this fire of the Holy Ghost] be ever frozen and cooled, and overmuch founded and rooted in the love of ourselves.[5]

This passage, which concerns the "whole duty of man," is the Christian Gospel *in nuce.* The human person is caught up in himself and herself until set free to love by a prior exterior love. That love is the forgiving love of Christ Jesus, without which all human endeavors of love are doomed to be scripted from need and projection. Christ's love engenders human love, and not ever the other way around. The tree must first be sound before its fruit can be sound, and good. The divine love precedes the human love, and not ever the reverse.

This passage is exactly equivalent to innumerable passages in Luther concerning God's prior love. The passage is equivalent also, idea for idea, to several passages in Tyndale and also in Cranmer's first two homilies of the Church of England.

The key insight found here, that non-self-interested acts of love are preceded by *the* act of love on Christ's part, which stills the human craving for appreciation and positive regard, is the material principle of the Protestant Reformation. It is encapsulated in the phrase "justification (by grace) through faith." It is this *material* or inward principle that lies behind the *formal* or outward principle of Anne Boleyn's reign as queen. The formal principle of Anne's reign was: "Burn down the Mission" (Elton John). In other words, get rid

5. Quoted in Ives, *Anne Boleyn,* 322-23.

of the externals that support the *opposite* material principle, the principle of gaining God's affirmation by deeds of veneration and visible devotion.

It is not always realized that Anne and Thomas Cromwell and Thomas Cranmer and their supporters and associates were destructive out of a consuming desire to redirect the nation's piety away from *works*, and towards *love*, in order to *inspire works*. On this theological/ideological foundation, Anne stood foursquare with all the "Lutherans" of her age.

The evangelical or Protestant position in the early years of the Reformation emphasized the inwardness of true religion (St. Matthew 15:17-20; St. Mark 7:14-23) in opposition to outward or "formal" religion. The *material* principle of the Reformation, I repeat, was the essence or substance of this: justification (by grace) through faith. The *formal* principle of the Reformation was the outward or visible form taken by the material principle: the husk in distinction to the kernel. Thus Scripture alone *(sola Scriptura)* is the *formal* principle of the Reformation, while its *material* principle is God's grace *(sola gratia)* responded to by means of faith *(sola fide)*.

Anne's religion is well expressed through the Ecclesiastes commentary. It is perfectly summarized in the verse from St. John's Gospel imprinted on the back binding of her French Bible. That verse, from its late first-century source, speaks for the entire primavera moment of the Reformation spring: The law has given way to grace. "Lo, the winter is past, . . . the flowers appear on the earth, the time of singing has come" (Song of Solomon 2:11, 12).

No ONE can know how Anne's emphases in theology might have developed or changed had she lived past the age of thirty. Maybe they would have undergone no changes. The logic of Reformation thought was to move from the insight of justification, to the question of mediation, that is, how is Christ's presence on earth encountered? In particular, how does the material principle of grace relate to the formal "clothing" of the sacraments, specifically to the bread and wine of the Mass. These would be the questions addressed by the women in the second phase of the Reformation, specifically Anne Askew and Jane Grey. The third phase, as addressed by Catherine Willoughby, would struggle with the question of God's providence, but that was still several years away.

No clearer textbook of early English Protestant principle was ever written than William Tyndale's 1534 preface to his translation of the Epistle to the Romans from Greek into English. Most of it was actually a translation by Tyndale of Luther's 1522 preface to Romans. But Tyndale's focus on the works of the law versus faith working through love is emblematic for everything his contemporary Anne read and acted out during her years as Henry's queen. Tyndale's prose condenses the thought of Anne:

> Mine own works can never satisfy the law or pay her what I owe her. For I owe the law to love her with all mine heart, soul, power and might. Which thing to pay I am never able. . . . No, I cannot once begin to love the law, except that I be first sure by faith that God loveth me and forgiveth me.[6]

INTERPRETATION

Anne Boleyn's copy of Tyndale's New Testament, now to be seen in the British Library at London, attests to the substance of her religion. As a theological person, she did not go beyond Tyndale's great monocular emphasis: the priority, in time, of God's grace before the possibility of the human being's grace to another human being. This was Luther's insight, that divine love engenders loving

---

6. *Tyndale's New Testament,* in a modern-spelling edition and with an introduction by David Daniell (New Haven: Yale University Press, 1989).

and not that our love stimulates the divine love. Anne might have gone further, in the direction of criticizing the church's eucharistic theology, had she lived longer. There is no evidence for this, however. Anne was part of the first generation of English Reformers and can be classified aptly with Robert Barnes, Thomas Bilney, Patrick Hamilton, and John Frith, as well as with the French vanguard, Jacques Lefèvre d'Étaples and Marguerite de Navarre.

EACH of the five women discussed in this book can be assigned a contemporary soul mate within the Reformation movement, and also a nemesis. Anne's soul mate was William Tyndale. When he was strangled publicly on October 6, 1536, his last words declared his cause and also his loyalty to the English king: "God, open the King of England's eyes."

Anne's last words on the scaffold the same year declared a similar loyalty:

> Good Christian people, I have not come here to preach a sermon; I have come here to die. . . . For according to the law and by the law I am judged I die, and therefore I will speak nothing against it. I am come hither to accuse no man, nor to speak of that whereof I am accused . . . but I pray God save the king and send him long to reign over you, for a gentler nor a more merciful prince was there never. . . ."

Yet Anne did, finally, have a nemesis. Her nemesis, on the long view, was her own love and husband, the very named Henry Tudor. Henry wooed Anne, though we would today say that the wooing was consensual (Anne wanted to be Henry's queen). He made her what she became. He fell out with her, within himself, when she could not produce a future king. His eye it was that roved, in the direction of Jane Seymour — although Jane, too, with her family, was intensely ambitious. In the end, it was Henry who believed the fictitious reports of adultery and collusion. It was Henry who permitted Cromwell and the others to turn the coup that brought down Anne in hours flat. Henry refused to see her then nor listen to any other view. It was Henry who forced Cranmer across the river at Lambeth to declare their marriage null and void on account of her "adultery." And it was Henry who married Jane within the closest possible span of time after Anne's execution.

Was it gender that undid Anne? Was it power? Was Anne a martyr to the power of the male over the female? Was sex her tool and also her self-inflicted prison? Was it a reciprocal gender dynamic, male and female, for which both Henry and Anne were jointly responsible? Or was it theology? Did Anne come too close to the illicit flame of subversive ideas emanating from Luther and from his English pupil William Tyndale?

Anne did not see herself principally as a Christian martyr.[7] She saw herself as a person who had gambled with very high stakes and lost. But as queen, Anne understood her providential mission to be this: to bring the Reformation to England and employ every single instance of patronage and influence to that end. Her self-confidence and bearing aided the Protestant cause immeasurably. In fact it was through Anne that the New Religion entered England.

Yet in the end Anne became a victim, and her life was tragic. "The whole creation has been groaning in travail together until now; and not only the creation, but we ourselves" (Romans 8:22-23).

---

7. Her brother George did. His speech at the scaffold suggests it, although it also includes striking words of self-criticism.

Chapter Two

ANNE ASKEW

(1521-1546)

There was at the same time also burnt together with her one Nicolas Belenian priest of Shropshire, John Adams, a tailor, and John Lasselles Gentleman of the Court and household of King Henry. . . .

It happened well for them, that they died together with Anne Askew. For albeit that of themselves they were strong and stout men, yet through the example and prayer of her, they being the more boldened, received occasion of more greater comfort, in that so painful and doleful kind of death, not only beholding her invincible constancy, but also oftentimes stirred up through her persuasions, they did set apart all kind of fear.[1]

HER LIFE IN BRIEF

The families who championed the Reformed cause in its first beachhead in England came very quickly to know one another and

---

1. From John Foxe's *Acts and Monuments* (1563), as quoted in *The Examination of Anne Askew*, edited by Elaine V. Beilin (New York: Oxford University Press, 1996), 192.

also to support one another. Thus Anne Askew's sister married George St. Paul, who administered Catherine Willoughby's estate. Moreover, Anne's brother became part of Thomas Cranmer's household. Anne herself, whose family was lesser nobility, became attached to the ladies-in-waiting of Katharine Parr, Henry VIII's sixth wife. Catherine Willoughby was among those ladies-in-waiting before Anne joined the circle. Then after Henry's death in 1546, Katharine Parr took Jane Grey under her wing, when Jane was only nine years old. They were a tight circle.

It is an amazing fact that when Anne Askew was tortured on the rack on June 29, 1546, she refused to give away the names of any of that group, as heretics and hence traitors to Henry, and thus stood fully firm in her confession. This was despite the fact that several of her bones were dislocated and some broken. Three weeks later she was carried to the stake in a chair.

The point is, these women were loyal to each other right up to the point of death. That is no overstatement. The accession of Elizabeth I in 1559 brought the story full circle, for Elizabeth had been a young child within the "extended family" of this group. Elizabeth herself was a more worldly person than our Bible-study sisterhood, by whose efforts her success was partly achieved.

Anne Askew, Katharine Parr, Jane Grey, and Catherine Willoughby can be compared justly to a chapter of Women Aglow in a town like Locust Valley, Long Island, or to a close-knit fellowship of "Bible-study moms" in Potomac, Maryland. The same dynamics, the same conscious, overriding commitment to the Lord and to the Scripture and to one another, apply. The difference is simply that the Tudor women were few in number, their work was illegal, and their hopes extended directly to the White House, i.e., the Royal Palace, and through the White House to the nation.

Anne was married to Thomas Kyme, of whom nothing is known save that he was sent for later from Lincoln to testify against Anne in London. In fairness to Kyme, he was not summoned so much to betray her as to intimidate her and take her home. His contrived intervention was exactly like the importation of the Mafioso's mother, flown in from Sicily to the congressional hearing on Capitol Hill, in the movie *Godfather II*.

Anne repudiated her marriage and stood on II Corinthians 6:14: "Be not unequally yoked with an unbeliever." She also got in trouble with the clergy of Lincoln Cathedral for reading her English Bible sitting solitarily in the back of the nave, and for rebuking them sharply when they tried to rebuke her. There is a parallel here to William Tyndale, who right at the earliest stage of his career offended his fellow clergy near Bristol. Their antipathy, both in Tyndale's case and in Askew's case, foreshadowed the events that took place a few years later on a larger canvas.

We know nothing about Anne's person except what she reveals about herself in the account she wrote of her two examinations and in her confessions of faith that were recorded in connection with her three arrests of March 1545, June 1545, and June 1546. She was condemned on June 28, and racked on June 29, after the political stakes involved in Queen Katharine Parr's religious views suddenly skyrocketed in the light of King Henry's grave illness. Anne Askew was burned at the stake on July 16, 1546. An eyewitness account of her death survives. This is by John Louth, who was archdeacon of Nottingham.

Anne's personality and temperament, unlike that of Anne Boleyn, is revealed vividly in the *Examinations*. She is sarcastic and provocative, solomonic and discreet, fearless but never bluffing; intellectually consistent; wily but also strong and forward; answerable to no one save her conscience before the Christ of the Scriptures; somewhat fanatical, one has to say (though events vindicated her); and as unwaveringly courageous as any figure we could name from the Reformation period. Her closing motto, "Pray, pray, pray," an exclamation repeated twice during the darkest hour, is extremely moving. She also appeals to her gender on several occasions, but invariably in the sense of "Why are you learned men getting so riled up over such a weak and silly woman as I?"

THE TEXTS

Anne's *Examinations*, written in her own hand, were published by John Bale in 1546 and 1547, almost immediately after the interrogations they report. Bale, a committed English Protestant churchman in exile in Germany, had them printed there. Later, when it was safe to publish them in England, John Foxe included them in his 1563 history of the English Reformation known as *The Acts and Monuments*. The "Ballad of Anne Askew" was published as early as 1596. It is possible but unproven that she wrote it herself. There is also an "Epitaph in Sapphic Verse," which John Foxe wrote to accompany a second edition of the *Examinations*.

A section of Foxe's "Epitaph" is quoted here, because Foxe understands fully the implications of the protection, and consequent delay and reprieve, which Anne's stance won for Queen Katharine and thus for the Protestant succession. This translation of Foxe's Latin is by G. P. Gould.

Her piety shines forth the brighter for being subjected to torture;/nor does she waver in truth for any fear/of chains: rather do these sooner wear out and fall apart.

The executioner comes forth, seething with ruthless frenzy:/her tendons untied, the woman lies tied up to make her/betray her partners in religion.

But she divulges no name, and by her silence the woman proves/stronger than the machine. They stand dumbstruck, and are/driven mad by the delay: yet they achieve nothing.

Her limbs are forced apart, her bones are broken, severed/
from their joints; nothing in that chaste body is left intact./
Still one part of her defeats the tyrants.

For her tongue alone could not be moved by any suffering:/
in rescuing her companions from her own peril, she bids/
them slumber with untroubled ears.

HER THEOLOGY

Anne Askew's theological emphases are different from Anne
Boleyn's. They reappear almost word for word in Jane Grey's incautious and exceptionally public words to Lady Anne Wharton
outside Mary Tudor's private (Catholic) chapel, which were repeated back to her during the examination at the Tower of London
by John Feckenham on February 10, 1554. Anne Askew's primary
target was biblical teaching concerning the Eucharist, and more
precisely the idea of transubstantiation. Anne was burned for denying transubstantiation. Her denial of it was aggressive. In fact
she mocked the concept!

What is different in Askew and Grey as compared to Anne
Boleyn is the focus on the Mass. The first phase of Reformation
theology was justification by grace through faith *rediscovered*.
The second phase was the *implications* of justification by faith for
the Mass, the Mass being the central action and transaction of
medieval Catholicism. The third phase of the English Reformation was the focus on election and predestination. This we shall
observe beginning to come to the fore in the letters of Catherine
Willoughby.

Anne's examination consisted mostly of attempts by "learned"
interrogators to get her to "out" her ideas concerning the sacrament (i.e., the Mass). Here is a typical example of what took place:

He [the chief examiner, whose name was Christopher Dare] sent for a priest to examine me. . . . The priest asked me, what I said to the Sacrament of the altar? But I desired him again, to hold me excused concerning that matter. None other answers would I make him, because I perceived him a papist.

Besides this my Lord mayor layed one thing under my charge, which was never spoken of me, but of them. And that was, whether a mouse eating the host, received God or no? This question did I never ask, but indeed they asked it of me, wherewith I made them no answer, but smiled!

In 1890, Bishop J. C. Ryle of Liverpool asked, rhetorically, an important question: "Why were our Reformers burned?" He understood that the main Protestant leaders were not tried for securing or reading the Bible in the vernacular, nor for their teaching concerning grace and faith. The Reformers were burned because they denied transubstantiation. This was the charge that stuck. Accordingly, almost all the hostile questions that were asked of Anne narrowed down to this one: Do you deny the "real presence," or corporeal presence, of Christ in the elements of the Eucharist?

Anne's denial of the "real presence" is seen in the confession of faith which she made at Newgate Prison shortly before her execution. Her denial is both negative and positive.

There be some do say, that I deny the eucharist or sacrament of thanksgiving. But those people do untruly report of me. For I both say and believe it, that if it were ordered, like as Christ instituted it, and left it, a most singular comfort it were unto us all. But as concerning your mass, as it is now used in our days, I do say and believe it, to be the most abominable idol that is in the world. For my God will not be eaten with teeth, neither yet dieth he again. And upon these words, that I have now spoken, will I suffer death.

Anne has two reasons for rejecting the Catholic view of the Mass. First, it is irrational to say that God can be contained within any object of any kind. Here Anne saw herself as a contemporary of Stephen, who said in Acts that the Most High does not dwell in houses made with hands (8:48). St. Paul said the same thing to the Athenians in Acts 17. Anne ridicules pitilessly the idea that any object of observation can coincide with God's "body"!

I cannot believe what I cannot see and "God will not be eaten with teeth": This is the Enlightenment or critical, deconstructing side of Protestantism in early form. Church historians call it "Zwinglian" or "Swiss." I see it as the spirit behind the son's remark to his father that the emperor has no clothes.

In addition to her appeal to common sense and observation, however, Anne has a deeper, more *evangelical* reason for faulting the Mass. She repudiates eucharistic sacrifice!: "Neither yet dieth he again." Central to Reformation theology was the one atoning sacrifice of Christ upon the cross for the sin (original sin) and the sins of the whole world. To conceive of the Eucharist as a sacrifice of repetition, by which the benefits of Christ's death are presented new and actual each time on the altar, was to denigrate the "one, full perfect sacrifice, satisfaction, and oblation for the sins of the whole world" (Cranmer's words). The Reforming interest saw the idea of eucharistic sacrifice, or better, the repetition of Christ's sacrifice in the Eucharist, as taking away from the one thing in Christianity you can count on amid the ambiguities of the human present. The past sacrifice, complete in itself, is grasped by inward trust, not visible reenactment. Anne Askew said this at least twice during her examinations. "Should we rather believe in private masses, than in the healthsome death of the dear son of God?"

There is more to Anne's theology, such as her sole reliance on

Scripture to prove her points. She proof-texts but she is also almost always on solid ground. She rarely says anything that is inherently eccentric. Her main eccentricity is the tactic by which she sometimes refers to herself as a "poor" or "weak" or "mere" woman. This is a smokescreen which contributes nothing to her argument, although it does discomfit her male examiners. Anne also infuriates the priests when she says she will gladly believe all that is taught in the catholic faith and by the catholic church while obviously using "catholic" in the sense of universal or creedal rather than Roman.

If Anne had conceded but one point, that "the sacrament be flesh, blood, and bone," she would have been released. Bishop Gardiner of Winchester pressed her to make that simple statement, after which "all would be well." She refused and, unfortunately for her, was kept in jail long enough for King Henry's health to decline dramatically and for the royal succession to be at stake. The question became suddenly less theological than political: Would Henry's young son Edward be given Protestant-minded tutors and a Protestant regent or would he be given Catholic tutors and a Catholic regent? Everything depended on the answer to that question.

The Catholic party at court knew that the queen, Katharine Parr, was an articulate, convinced Protestant, sheltering many other convinced Protestants "beneath her skirts." If Henry could be persuaded himself, by evidence extracted from Catherine's friend Anne Askew, that the queen was the tool of Protestant *political* interests, Henry might throw the succession over to the Catholics. Thus Anne's being in prison coincided with a devoutly hoped-for *coup d'état* by the Catholic party. This was extremely bad news for Anne.

Theology in the examination room becomes instantly subordinated to the politics of state in the torture chamber. Would Anne have been burned as a result of her eucharistic theology alone? Under Henry, even Henry on the fence? Probably not. But once she was stretched and bent and broken and pulled half apart, she had to be gotten rid of. She had to become history.

As ANNE entered the last chapter of her life, beginning with her transfer to Newgate Jail, a new element comes into the narration. She starts closing her paragraphs with the words, "Pray, pray, pray." The piety is real and transparent. Ejaculatory prayers like this occur rarely among the Reformers, female and male. Their coinage more typically is that of reasoned argument and the massing of texts. Towards the end, however, Anne exhorts herself, and her readers, to do this one thing: "I sent the Lord Chancellor again word, that I would rather die than to break my faith. Then the Lord open the eyes of their blind hearts, that the truth may take place. Farewell, dear friend, and pray, pray, pray."

Anne's next-to-last words recorded before her torture by the state are quintessential. They sum up the plain approach of her practical reason:

> As for that you call your God, (it) is but a piece of bread. For a more proof thereof . . . , let it lie on the box but three months, and it will be mold, and so turn to nothing that is good. Whereupon I am persuaded, that it cannot be God.

INTERPRETATION

It is hard to read the examinations of Anne Askew without seeing a firebrand, a fanatic even, who was "asking for it." So out on a limb is Anne, so irritating to her opponents with her combination of irony, iron certainty, and the coyness of her appeals to be but a "poor, wee woman," that we have to ask whether she is not a great curiosity, a one-hit wonder of the English Reformation.

Anne bursts on the scene with her first arrest in March 1543, and is unlike anyone the Catholic side had dealt with before her. What are we to make of Anne Askew?

We are missing evidence concerning Anne's relation with her sisters among the Reformers in the circle of Katharine Parr. We know they were tightly knit from the picture Foxe gives of the conspiracy against Anne by the duke of Norfolk and Bishop Gardiner. We can imagine them quick-stowing their testaments — dropping the pills in the loo, so to speak — when Henry pays his famous personal visit on the queen to verify her "heresy." There they sit smiling, sunny and chatting innocently, all bent over their expected, accustomed needlework. But it is no hen party. They are all praying for their husbands, praying for their children, praying for the King, praying endlessly for wisdom in walking the tightrope, praying for Bible readers in secret, praying for the bishops (to be replaced), praying for Cranmer, praying for the schools, praying for the nation.

Anne is their brightest and their best, their big gun at argument, the "brain" in the group. Anne's mocking attitude towards most men isolated her just a little within her circle. But she is still the heavy artillery of the group.

What makes Anne memorable and irrepressible is her mind. It is a heat-seeking missile to explode the illogic and myth-building of the official medieval notion of sacrament. Anne is a dog with a bone on the issue of Scripture's sole authority in religion, on the unprovable abstraction of transubstantiation, and on the unique sacrifice of Christ to which nothing can be added.

We could call Anne single-minded, perhaps even a little superficial, but at the same time integrated. She reminds me of the teenage martyr to Hitler, Sophie Scholl, who told her mother how hungry she was for a good breakfast on the morning of her execution. It is as if Anne Askew were unable not to be transparent, right up to the final crisis:

Then they did put me on the rack, because I confessed no ladies or Gentle women to be of my opinion, and thereon they kept me a long time. And because I lay still and did not cry, my Lord chancellor and Master Rich, took pains to rack me with their hands, till I was nigh dead. Then the lieutenant caused me to be loosed from the rack. Incontinually. I swooned, and then they recovered me again. After that I sat two long hours reasoning with my Lord chancellor upon the bare floor, whereas he with many flattering words, persuaded me to leave my opinion. But my lord God (I thank his everlasting goodness) gave me grace to persevere and will do (I hope) to the very end . . . pray, pray, pray.

I defy the reader to be indifferent to these words. By any standard Anne Askew was a person drawn to the highest pitch of human courage.

As WITH Anne Boleyn, there were important men in Anne Askew's life. At least two of them make it possible to reflect on the relation of her achievement to her gender. Men like John Bale, Anne's posthumous partisan, draw the scorn of feminist interpreters such as Elaine Beilin, because men of Bale's ilk, publicists, are regarded as users. The charge is that Anne's particular form of self-expression, her specific witness, which was related somehow to her gender or at least to the suppression of her gender by power-wielding men, was used by John Bale as a sort of case-in-point. In their view, Anne Askew's story is one of conflict with authority, i.e., with men. Men like Bale had little feeling for Anne as a person, and certainly not for Anne as a woman. Anne's theological position, especially her martyrdom, simply suited his own agenda. John used Anne, in other words, as a tool to further his own ideology.

It is true that the Reformers typically used stories of other Reformers, especially of contemporary martyrs to the cause, to forward their case. John Foxe did this in England, Agrippa d'Aubigny did it in France, and Flavius Illyricus did it in Germany. Those three are the tip of the iceberg. *But it was not a gender ploy.* The Reformation chroniclers "used" many more men than women in their illustrative cases of the church under the cross. And the women used the men in the same way. Jane Grey idolized Heinrich Bullinger of Zürich. Anne Boleyn propped up Cranmer in every way she possibly could. She also used her power of patronage exclusively to put evangelical men into high position within the Church of England. Catherine Willoughby was much more strenuous an ideologue than her powerful, discreet protector and defender, William Cecil. Anne Askew's single-minded call to arms in Newgate Jail probably kept John Lassells from knuckling under to the same powerful men who broke her own body apart.

Anne Askew, in other words, was an ideological, agenda-driven person if there ever was one. I believe she would have understood John Bale to be the very best comrade in arms within the circumstances in which they both struggled.

Finally, on Bale, it is true that his glosses or comments on Anne's written replies to Gardiner and company are inordinately long, and certainly preachy. But if it had not been for John Bale, there is no guarantee at all that the notes she took of her astonishing examinations would ever have survived. Anne owes the survival of her voice, her woman's voice, to John Bale. He preserved that voice in print as a stranger in a strange land in Marburg, Germany. It is John Bale, moreover, who, less than one year after her death, placed this text from Proverbs 31 (verse 26) on the 1546 frontispiece of Anne's examinations, beneath a picture of *her* suppressing the papal dragon:

> Favor is deceitful and beauty is a vain thing. But a woman that feareth the Lord is worthy to be praised. She openeth her mouth to wisdom and in her language is the law of grace.

In the long view of history, it is not John Bale who used Anne, but Anne who used John Bale!

There is also, however, a male villain to this piece. It is not the torturer, Richard Rich, who was almost as horrible and devious to Sir Thomas More on the Catholic side, as he was to Anne, on the Protestant side. The villain of the piece is the same villain we saw as the "prowling lion" (I Peter 5:8) in Anne Boleyn's career. That villain is Henry Tudor.

Henry *claimed* to be interested in theology, but he was a dilettante, like James I. Henry *claimed* to be a courtly suitor and lover, but he was completely involved in himself and thought only of himself. Henry *claimed* to have only the best interests of the kingdom at heart, but he played off both ends against the middle from the first to the last day of his reign. I see Henry as a narcissist, a user, the "political animal" of his era. He may have had moments, even phases, of a higher calling, for at one point he really did feel he was defending English Christianity from the "wild boar" of Luther's heresy. He really did understand the potential cost to the nation of the nonexistence of a male heir, in the light of the horrific recent past of the Wars of the Roses. But the record reveals a character who threw his weight around in order to get his way.

By his shilly-shallying at the end — I believe he loved it! — between Protestant-minded and Catholic-minded guardians for his son, Henry created, again, an atmosphere of intrigue that ended up devouring one woman, though not Katharine Parr, who probably owed her life to Anne, nor Catherine Willoughby, who likewise could have been fearfully implicated. Henry's keeping everyone on edge right up to the last hours of his life created the situation in which the Catholic conspirators needed someone to confess and implicate the others. Anne Askew, herself completely uninterested in politics, solely interested in the Reformed Religion, was young, not so highly born as the others, and thus more expendable. Anne was also the more discardable because of her repudiated marriage to Kyme. On paper, Anne was supremely vulnerable to torture. The steel trap of high-stakes political intrigue that closed lethally over Anne was the creation of Henry. He is to blame for Anne's horrifying physical destruction.

The fact that the Reformation was preserved in England can be attributed to the amazing presence of mind, and maturity, of Katharine Parr, as we shall see in the next chapter. But Katharine Parr may not have had her chance without the strength and courage of her martyred lady-in-waiting. That great martyr was the iron magnolia, better, the Iron Giant: Anne Askew.

Chapter Three

KATHARINE PARR

(1514-1548)

HER LIFE IN BRIEF

Katharine Parr was taught early to know Latin, Greek, and French, also possibly Italian. She was a child in that golden window of time when noble women were educated according to the highest possible standard. The princesses Elizabeth and Mary, Lady Jane Grey, Anne Boleyn as we have already seen, Anne Askew a little less, and Catherine Willoughby, also less, were encouraged by their fathers and their private tutors to read the classics and also translate them. Because she was a child prodigy, Jane Grey excelled them all. But Katharine's written work reveals an extremely intelligent and organized mind.

Her first two husbands died, and she was married to King Henry VIII in July 1543, thus becoming Henry's sixth queen. One of her attendants that day was Catherine Willoughby.

Katharine Parr is often portrayed as the prescient handler of an extremely difficult and unpredictable man, a motherly character rubbing her husband's bad leg and soothing his temper with soft words. That picture of Katharine is, to put it mildly, short of the truth. She had presence of mind, maturity, and intelligence; she knew how not to lose her head — in both senses.

Katharine did, however, miss one vital signal in her relationship with Henry. That fact shows that she was not a highly calculating person. Only a stroke of luck — providence! — alerted her to the storm clouds gathering around her.

Her primary motivation was the New Religion, the Reformation cause. Her recorded words and her incomparable book *Lamentation of a Sinner,* written when she was Queen of England, reveal her true interest. The title that Katharine was given by later writers, "nursing mother of the Reformation," is correct.

The description from the previous chapter of Katharine's court circle stowing their (banned) Bibles and blithely looking up like the Stepford Wives when the *Stasi* walked in, is a true one. It goes back to an incident which occurred in 1546, Henry's last year of life, and which is splendidly represented in detail by John Foxe. Foxe's account is regarded by all historians as true, even while his own point of view (i.e., as Protestant chronicler) is obvious to the reader.

What happened is this: the Catholic party at court were desperately worried that Henry at his death would tilt the succession to the Protestants by designating a Protestant protector or regent for the boy-king, Edward. Edward was Henry's son by Jane Seymour. The Catholics were led by the duke of Norfolk and Bishop Stephen Gardiner of Winchester — two names which will recur in the histories of our women, for, as we have seen, the Tudor world was small — and the Lord Chancellor of England, Thomas Wriothesley, together with Richard Rich, racked Anne Askew. The Catholic party was unscrupulous. This is not to whitewash the Protestants, although the Protestants were more often on the defensive and accustomed to treading lightly.

The Catholics saw their moment when by chance Bishop Gardiner overheard a conversation in which Katharine Parr was arguing a point concerning the reformation of the church *with her hus-*

band Henry himself. Gardiner noticed that the king became irritated. John Foxe explains, rightly I think, that Henry was in physical pain. His wick was short for one of Katharine's harangues, as he surely received it that day, on the subject of theology. Gardiner actually heard Henry say as he walked out of the room, "A good hearing it is when women become clerks (i.e., clergy); and a thing much to my comfort, to come in mine old days to be taught by my wife!"

There is some theater to all this, some "soap opera," even a little of Lucy and Desi. But it was not funny, in fact. Gardiner was able to take that remark and insinuate to Henry that his wife was a heretic and was trying to engineer through Henry a radical version of Reform that could well amount to treason. The bishop said that it was possible the king was "cherishing a serpent in his bosom." Henry then implied to Gardiner that he would listen if Gardiner were able to draw up concrete charges against the queen. These charges would have to accuse Katharine of denying one or more of the (Catholic) Six Articles, which Henry had promulgated both to appease the Catholic party and to suppress the "left wing" (as he understood it) of the Reform. Gardiner moved, like a cat, with extreme speed. Katharine knew nothing of what was coming.

Fortunately, providentially, a sheet of paper with the coming accusations scrawled on it somehow fell out of the pocket of one of the orchestrators. This paper was picked up by a Protestant — we have no idea by whom — and passed to Katharine. Katharine turned white, grasping the whole picture in exactly five seconds. How had she missed it after Henry's body language had betrayed it just a few days before to the more subtle Gardiner? Katharine's surprise puts her in a somewhat unworldly light.

She had an anxiety attack on the spot. The king was immediately informed of the queen's fit. He sent one of his personal physicians, Dr. Wendy (no kidding), a closet Protestant, to see Katharine. Dr. Wendy helped compose Katharine and encouraged her that all was not lost. He exhorted her to stop and *think*, and figure out the wisest and most prudential course.

Then comes the famous moment, it can accurately be said, in which Katharine was given to save the Reformation in England. She collected herself, and the following night visited the king "in his chamber," accompanied by her sister Lady Herbert, another "sister" in the cause. This is what she said. It was remembered by the six or seven witnesses and written down immediately afterwards:

> Your Majesty doth right well know, neither I myself am ignorant, what great imperfection and weakness by our first creation, is allotted unto us women, to be ordained and appointed as inferior and subject unto men as our head, from which head all our direction ought to proceed, and that as God made man to his own shape and likeness, whereby he being endued with more special gifts of perfection, might rather be stirred to the contemplation of heavenly things, and to the earnest endeavor to obey his commandments; even so also made he woman of man, of whom and by whom she is to be governed, commanded, and directed. Where womanly weakness and natural imperfection, ought to be tolerated, aided, and borne without, so that by his wisdom such things as are lacking in her, ought to be supplied.

And so it went. At the end of this speech, the king said, "And is it even so, sweetheart? And tended your arguments to no worse end? Then perfect friends we are again, as ever at any time heretofore." Then he kissed her, and that was that, save a final coda.

WHAT a performance! There are at least two things to be said about it. First, I have no doubt that Katharine's words to the king were as Foxe reports them. This is because the rhetoric, especially the repetition of phrases, and of verbs in particular, is typical of her style in her book *Lamentation of a Sinner.* On stylistic grounds alone the speech sounds like Katharine. Second, it is a rare and atypical appeal to a woman's "station," which she clearly fashioned to appeal to Henry's pride. Flattery will get you everything! One could say that her appeal to his (male) ego was outrageous and shameless, and also insincere. But her remarks, really her bold apology, were the result of collected thought for the sake of the "one thing needful" (St. Luke 10:32). We say today, love has no pride. Translate that in Katharine's case: Love for the cause, really for the Christ, can have no limit of self-denigration and self-disparagement.

By our standards today, Katharine Parr humiliated herself before her husband. Obviously to her, it was a small price to pay to protect the Reformed Religion. In actuality, we know that she regarded Henry in his better moments as the new Moses to England, leading his country out of Egypt (i.e., Catholicism) under threat of Pharaoh (i.e., the Bishop of Rome).[1] The fact remains that the queen's image before the world, and certainly before her difficult husband, was subordinate in her mind to the claim of Christ on her life. I use her own thought forms to describe her, the categories she herself would have accepted.

To conclude the story: just a few days later, the axe fell, supposedly. And it veered sharply off, rebounding on the predators. Norfolk and the Lord Chancellor entered a principal chamber where

---

1. "Our Moses, and most godly wise governor and king, hath delivered us out of captivity and bondage of Pharaoh. I mean by this Moses, king Henry the Eighth, my most sovereign favorable lord and husband. . . . And I mean by this Pharaoh, the bishop of Rome, who hath been, and is a greater persecutor of all true Christians, than ever was Pharaoh of the children of Israel; for he is a persecutor of the gospel and grace, a setter forth of all superstition and counterfeit holiness, bringing many souls to hell with his alchemy and counterfeit mercy . . . the Lord keep and defend all men from his jugglings and sleights, but especially the poor, simple, and unlearned souls" (Katharine Parr, *Lamentation of a Sinner,* p. 50).

Katharine was, in the company of the king. Everything was to be public. The conspirators were followed by a troop of soldiers carrying halberds. But when Henry observed them from the corner of his eye, as they waited anxiously to one side, his face turned grim. He excused himself from Katharine, strode quietly over to the men, and then gave them a piece of his mind! How dare they have filled his mind with malicious fictions and deceit. He dismissed them absolutely. We read that the plotters retired in dismay. Henry then wheeled back and addressed the queen to this effect: "Now where were we, darling?"

Henry never trusted the duke of Norfolk and Bishop Gardiner again. The boomerang was total. When he died, Henry assigned the sincere Protestant Protector Somerset — in contrast to the *insincere* Protestant Protector Northumberland — to govern for Edward. Just before he died, Henry accepted Cranmer's ministry to the depth of his soul, "trusting to Jesus alone." This is exactly what happened. It was Katharine's brilliant achievement.

HENRY made no provision for Katharine after his death. She exited the royal household noiselessly, with almost no further mention in the histories. What happened to her subsequently is sad and touching.

Sir Thomas Seymour, who carried the more or less meaningless title of Admiral of England, was a good-looking rogue. Katharine had liked him before she married Henry; he was sort of a "lost love" to her. Seymour really wanted to marry Princess Elizabeth, but he was accused, when Elizabeth was eleven or twelve years old, of child sexual abuse — child abuse in the modern sense. The charge was substantiated by one of Elizabeth's nurses who found them in an extremely compromising situation in the Princess's bedroom. Seymour was barred from ever seeing her again. The scandal of the situation forced Elizabeth to keep a very low profile during the entire reign of her half-brother, Edward VI. Seymour instead asked Katharine to marry him, as her fourth husband. Her unhesitating "yes," so soon after Henry's death, is usually explained as a product of an "old flame" she still carried, although it could also have been due to her need for a protector and provider.

Katharine died from an infection a few days after the birth of their child. She died at Sudeley Castle, near Tewkesbury, and save for grateful remembrance among the Elizabethan generation of Reformers who had struggled by her side, she was forgotten. In 1789 her coffin and bones were dug out from the ruins of the chapel building at Sudeley. They were reinterred, with pomp far in excess of what she would have wanted in life. Her tomb can now be visited by tourists in that theme park known as the Cotswolds. Today one can also see Katharine's intelligent, self-possessed, and soulful features in a painting at the National Portrait Gallery. Sir Roy Moore believed that this portrait of Henry's sixth queen was really a picture of Jane Grey. More recently, it has been proven without doubt that the picture is of Katharine. This is because the jewelry she is wearing matches exactly a list that has come down of her personal effects.

Katharine's *actual* interment, days after her death, tells a tale with which we can conclude this account of her life. Her chaplain, Miles Coverdale, who for his Protestantism was soon to have to flee to Germany and Switzerland during Queen Mary's reign, preceded the casket into the chapel in the late afternoon, at dusk. Little Jane Grey, who had become Katharine's special trust at the end, followed the casket, carrying a single candle. A psalm was said, a lesson was read, and Coverdale preached. He had one point: Let us have no superstition here. She would not have wanted it and it wouldn't be true anyway. We can thank God for His Christ and for the hope we Christians have. We commend this woman our sister in sure and certain hope. Then they left.

THE TEXTS

Katharine's book was published in the last years of her life by funds from her brother William, the Marquess of Northampton, and funds from (the ubiquitous) Catherine Willoughby. The introduction to the book, which is strong Gospel stuff, was composed by William Cecil, the famous Lord Burleigh, who later became so influential under Queen Elizabeth and in the meantime proved himself a deft survivor under Mary Tudor. The full title of the book is *Lamentation or Complaint of a Sinner Made by the Most Virtuous and Right Gracious Lady Queen Katharine, (Parr,) Bewailing the Ignorance of Her Blind Life, Led by Superstition.* The subtitle reads: *Very Profitable to the Amendment of Our Lives.*

The book is divided into twelve chapters. It is easy to follow and also easy to read in short doses, for purposes of daily meditation or reflection. The language is lucid and several times easier for the twenty-first-century reader than John Donne is, or Richard Hooker. The text is full of Katharine's characteristic verbs, hammering home her points in triplicate. Although at first reading a few years ago, my eyes glazed over as the text started to sound like a "generic" early-Reformation confession — there exist several self-styled autobiographical windows into the soul from contemporary Protestant thinkers — further and closer reading over time has disclosed jewels, both of substance and of style.

I write here as one who already agrees with almost everything Katharine says, and who is by theology entirely sympathetic with her understanding of Christianity. I become just a little uneasy only when Katharine invokes the vision of eternal hell. I have become too much of a modern not to wince when she quotes Christ's own words about the turn of the screw in unquenchable fire. The point is that for me as interpreter, Katharine's well-organized exposition of the law, i.e., that under which she understands herself to have lived before her conversion, and of grace, under which she believes she now lives, falls on my open ears and sympathetic inclinations. I wonder if any reader at all of this book from the year 1548 would have been other than sympathetic. But today, as with most Christian literature, who would actually wish to read such a book who was not already willing to relate to the description of being a sinner? No one else could possibly wish to take it down from the shelf!

Katharine Parr left behind a further text. It is a short collection of *Prayers and Meditations; Wherein the Mind is Stirred Patiently to Suffer all Afflictions Here, to set at Naught the Vain Propensity of this World, and Always to Long for the Everlasting Felicity.* There is nothing in these pages that conflicts with a single sentence and sentiment of the *Lamentation.* They are presented as a compilation "out of certain holy works by the most virtuous and gracious Princess Katharine, Queen of England, France and Ireland." The prayers in fact are mostly compiled or paraphrased from *The Imitation of Christ* by Thomas à Kempis. They cover twelve pages of text. I give one of them here, a typical representative:

> Make me, wretched sinner, obediently to use myself after thy will in all things, and patiently to bear the burden of this corruptible life. For though this life be tedious, and as a heavy burden for my soul, yet, nevertheless, through thy grace, and by example of thee, it is now much much more easy and comfortable, than it was before thy incarnation and passion. . . . O Lord Jesus, make that possible, by grace, which is impossible to me, by nature.

HER THEOLOGY

Katharine's *Lamentation* is a digest of early Reformation convictions about the self, the Gospel message to the self, and the attitude the converted self is able to adapt toward the world. After embracing the message of Christ's forgiveness, the self understands the exterior reality of life in a deconstructed, even adversarial way. This new vision of exterior reality breathes through every word of Katharine's dense and telescoped excursion into the psychology of the converted person. The sentiments breathe a reality that derives from personal experience. Moreover, William Cecil's introduction, written before he disappeared into the woodwork under Mary, is a surprisingly pure statement of evangelical truth from such a worldly-wise man.

The first chapter declares Katharine's repentance for her earlier life. No personal details of any kind are given, but a general picture is drawn:

> Christ was innocent, and void of all sin; and I wallowed in filthy sin, and was free from no sin. Christ was obedient unto his Father . . . and I disobedient, and most stubborn, even to the confession of truth. . . . Christ despised the world, with all the vanities thereof, and I made it my god, because of the vanities. Christ came to serve his brethren, and I coveted to rule over them. Christ despised worldly honour, and I much delighted to attain the same. . . . By this declaration, all creatures may perceive how far I was from Christ, and without Christ. (35-36)

Chapter two describes Katharine's conversion to the Christ of the Gospel:

> What! shall I fall in desperation? Nay, I will call upon Christ, The Light of the world. The Fountain of life, the Relief of all careful consciences, the Peacemaker between God and man, and the only health and comfort of all repentant sinners. (36)

Chapter three gives Katharine the chance to witness artlessly to her heartfelt feeling:

> I have certainly no curious learning to defend this mat-
> ter . . . , but a simple zeal and earnest love to the truth in-
> spired of God, who promiseth to pour his Spirit upon all
> flesh; which I have, by the grace of God, . . . felt in myself to
> be true. (41)

Katharine now proceeds in chapters four, five, and six to say what Christ has done, what his life and death imply and mean:

> When I look upon the Son of God . . . , so unarmed, naked,
> given up, and alone, with humility, patience, liberatingly,
> modesty, gentleness, and with all other his divine virtues,
> beating down to the ground all God's enemies, and making
> the soul of man so fair and beautiful; I am forced to say that
> his victory and triumph are marvellous; and therefore Christ
> well deserved to have this noble title, Jesus of Nazareth,
> King of the Jews. (43)

She magnifies the Lord with exhilarating successions of nouns and verbs.

In chapter seven she composes an encomium to Henry her hus-band, which today sounds nauseating. She then proceeds to docu-ment the "fruits of infidelity" and the offenses of "weaklings" and of "carnal gospellers," by whom she means those who take advantage of the grace of God to live undisciplined, immoral lives. What Kath-arine is in touch with here is the *simul iustus et peccator* concept, the idea that the Christian self is forever marred and compelled by hu-man nature, the inherited condition of self-will, self-involvement, and self-deception that wars chronically and perpetually against the high calling of the crucified repentant life. Katharine is sublimely aware of the already-and-not-yet condition of the Christian self, by which the hope of salvation is full *in spe* (i.e., in hope) but not yet fully *in re* (i.e., in actuality). She has no illusions about what the Reformers termed "concupiscence": the desire of the self to have its way, the desire that never finally fully gives ground until death. She writes towards the conclusion of her closing twelfth chapter: ". . . Alas! self-love doth so much reign among us, that, as I have said before, we cannot espy our own faults."

The *Lamentation* ends on an eschatological note. The day of the final judgment, to which her hearers will all be subject, is warningly described:

> We shall have no man of law to make our plea for us, neither can we have the day deferred; neither will the Judge be corrupted with affection, bribes, or reward; neither will he hear any excuse or delay; neither shall this saint, or that martyr, help us, be they ever so holy; neither shall our ignorance save us from damnation; but yet wilful blindness, and obstinate ignorance, shall receive greater punishment, and not without just cause. Then shall it be known who hath walked in the dark. (64)

To THE reader who does not feel to some degree what Katharine feels about herself, about the goodness of Christ, hence about the ultimate goodness of life given that great and singular exterior reference point; about the inherently clawing character of original sin continuing on in the Christianized self; and about the ultimate vindication of all that is good, as well as the ultimate requiting punishment of all that is bad; to such a reader, the *Lamentation*, if it is ever read at all, must be an incomprehensible, maybe even a dreadful contribution to the world's literature. Katharine is a "true believer," to use a phrase by which the secular world consigns committed religious feeling to the rack of fanaticism.

To the Christianized ear, on the other hand, or to the ear of anyone who is simply disillusioned by the world's ever-changing moods, Katharine's book will come across as true to experience, accurate in diagnosis, grateful in the heart's response to prior love, and unerringly correct in its warnings to self-deception both Christian and non-Christian. The *Lamentation* is actually less fierce than Jane Grey ever was, who held exactly the same convictions as Katharine but who was more than ten years younger when her own sentiments were transcribed. Moreover, Katharine writes like Richard Hooker, though better than Hooker, because her style is less lapidary and more lucid, less literary and more vocal than the styles in fashion at the end of that century.

Compare Katharine's "prose sermon" with John Donne's sermons. Her words are never unclear, her sentences never obscure. To my interpretation, she writes as directly as Luther, although she lacks his genius for unceasing new ideas and metaphors. Her approach is also less personal or directly autobiographical than Luther's, probably because, as the queen, she felt she needed to keep any personal anecdotes to herself. In fact, only her inflated words regarding her husband Henry set her work in a particular time and place.

INTERPRETATION

At least four men played decisive roles in the life of Katharine Parr: Henry Tudor, Miles Coverdale, William Cecil Lord Burleigh, and Thomas Seymour. The first and the last were vain and terrible. The second and the third were sacrificial and kind. That opinion sounds "un-nuanced," but I feel sure that if we had Katharine Parr to talk to right now, like the seated dead of *Our Town*, she would agree.

William Cecil was Katharine's good angel. Like John Bale to Anne Askew, Cecil was the medium through whom Katharine's message was published. He was more worldly than Bale and rode out the Marian succession while the other Reformers suffered on both sides of the Channel. But he was the Reformation's friend and was loyal to its female protagonists. His preface to Katharine's *Lamentation* is so heartfelt, so full of admiration and thanksgiving for his recent queen, and so unguarded in its statement of where he stands, that one cannot read it today without feeling for this man who went out of his way, together with the duchess of Suffolk and the marquess of Northampton, to put into print the testament of Katharine. For she wasn't exactly dropped when Henry died, but she had to clear the White House with a lot less fanfare than America's Bill Clinton did in January 2001. And there were no speaker's fees to come, no visiting lectureships, no book royalties, no product endorsements. It was William Cecil's help or nothing. I am sure this was not forgotten, neither by Katharine's friends nor by her many enemies. We also know that Cecil was *the* friend, the only friend, to Catherine Willoughby, who became a *persona non grata* in the eyes of Elizabeth Tudor. William Cecil was a constant friend to the Reforming women.

For Katharine Parr's evil genius, I would nominate Thomas Seymour. A narcissistic, selfish man, he was also to Katharine's mind her true love. We can readily understand the desire to catch just an hour or so of personal happiness, of personal fulfillment, in the world of responsibilities and obligations which governed Katharine's life from the earliest time. But if she thought she might find as Thomas Seymour's wife the personal fulfillment she had missed earlier, she was sadly wrong. Seymour cried when she died and apparently possessed real feelings for her. But he was a romantic adventurer even when she was carrying his child, whose birth brought on the sepsis that killed Katharine. Moreover, he did not share her faith and absented himself from the family chapel services she inaugurated at their home at Sudeley. Later, in a sermon before King Edward, Bishop Latimer called attention to Seymour's indifference to Katharine's religion. Not long after, Seymour was executed for treason. He wrote these words before he died, "Forgetting God to love a king, hath been my rod." That is not the half of it.

Lord Burleigh and Miles, later Bishop Coverdale, were Katharine's true friends; Henry VIII and Thomas Seymour, her false friends. So then, so also now. Only in hindsight can anyone know a person's true colors. In principle, however, based on the diagnosis of her own humanity in her great written achievement, *Lamentation of a Sinner,* and based upon her subtle unflappable stance in the court crisis of 1546, Katharine would have agreed. Only God can know a person's true colors. And it will all come to the light where there are no attorneys and no delays.

Chapter Four

JANE GREY

(1537-1554)

HER LIFE IN BRIEF

Or l'autre avec sa foy garda aussi le rang
D'un esprit tout royal, comme royal le sang.
Un royaume est pour elle, un autre Roy luy donne
Grace de mespriser la mortelle couronne
En cerchant l'immortelle, et luy donna les yeux
Pour troguer l'Angleterre au royaume des cieux:

. . .

Prisonniere ça bas, mais princesse là haut,
Elle changea son throne empour un eschafaut.

Agrippa d'Aubigné (1552-1630)
Les Tragiques, IV, 207-12, 215-16

Agrippa d'Aubigné was a French soldier who wrote an epic poem in seven books describing the (failed) Reformation in France. It is an almost unbearably tragic work and is aptly called *Les Tragiques.* I do not think it has ever been translated into English.

In Book IV of *Les Tragiques,* entitled *Les Feux,* or "The Fires" (of martyrdom), d'Aubigné pays rich homage to two of the subjects of this book. He narrates the tortures of Anne Askew, or "Askeuve" as he calls her. Then he proceeds to an ennobling elegy for the martyr queen, Jane Grey. The lines above say simply that she laid down her mortal crown for an immortal one in order to create out of England the kingdom of God! She thus exchanged her throne for a scaffold, in the spirit of Philippians 2:7-8.

Although the sixteen-year-old Jane Grey died during the reign of Bloody Mary, she was not rehabilitated in public memory under Elizabeth's Protestant reign. This was because the accusation against her, though a forced and contrived one, was treason; and treason was the most sensitive subject even under the *Protestant* Tudors.

The result of having this cloud over her memory was that interest in Jane did not finally flourish until the nineteenth century, during the reign of Queen Victoria. In the early 1800s Jane did in fact become a romantic figure, a tragic righteous hero, a victim of prideful intrigue on the part of Northumberland and her own mother, a reluctant bride who then fell in love with her equally victimized teenage husband, the martyred Nine Days Queen: a brilliant, bookish child prodigy turned Reformation legend.

Then in the last several decades, Jane again faded from view. Catholic historians like David Mathew and more recently a circle of English Catholic revisionists, led initially by Christopher Haigh, wished to represent her struggle as a purely political one. Her own theological views, they say, were a minor thread in a tapestry of so-called "Protestant" but really solely political Machiavellianism. The revisionists argue that the religious element was the least of the factors that brought about the Reformation's eventual public success. Much more important than theology — which was important only to a few "intellectuals" like Cranmer and his elite — were greed for monastic lands, English nationalism over against the Italian papacy, "new money" (i.e., "Protestant" mercantile) on the make for "old money" (i.e., "Catholic" agricultural), not to mention luck and the simple twists of fate that "really" govern history.

The repudiation of such a mechanistic and also oddly "serendipitous" view of the English Reformation, which is really just a newer form of partisan Catholicism among the academic historians, is both a very large task and an important new achievement. Fortunately, it is being done by writers such as Diarmaid MacCulloch and Ashley Null, among others. That essential work, of bringing the interpretation of the English Reformation back again in line with the texts that fired it, is beyond the scope of this short study. But reference to the background of "Jane Grey studies," for lack of a better term, brings me to my own, personal role in the story. Learning from feminist history, I wish to place my story in the setting of her story.

On a Sunday in 1985 the New York *Times* ran a feature about Trevor Nunn's about-to-be-released film *Lady Jane*. What caught my eye then was the director's statement that the movie dealt with a figure for whom the "religious controversies of her day" were the decisive thing. Ah, one thought, a modern movie that takes the Reformation seriously! Could such a thing be?

Such a thing was! *Lady Jane* is a serious, affecting piece. Yes, there are some Hollywood touches. Yes, the hippie-idealist side of Jane and Guilford is overdone. Yes, there is even some tasteful nudity the night before their deaths. But there is also a word-for-word depiction of Jane's debate with Dr. Feckenham, discussions with Dudley concerning justification by grace through faith, a mainly accurate reenactment of her famous being-discovered-alone-reading-Plato-in-Greek, and even the ominous encounter with Lady Ann Wharton outside Princess Mary's private chapel at Newhall in Essex. Add to it all a sublime musical score by Stephen Oliver, and *Lady Jane* is an artistic and also a religious success.

I saw it alone first, then took Mary, my wife, then took two of our small children. Then I saw it alone again. When the videotape was released later, I swallowed it whole. Then came the scholarly side, swallowing down every book I could find, near and far. Then a mid-winter, positively glacial pilgrimage to Bradgate Park, Jane's ruined house outside of Leicester, where I walked a whole day as the deer and I froze. I was "in love," hooked, moved. I was narcissus, too, for in Jane I discovered myself.

I saw reflected in Jane my own solitude as a child who had once been regarded as a prodigy. I saw Jane's isolation theologically, as an Episcopal minister who had always instinctively loved Martin Luther and his insight of grace by faith, or rather, unmerited love triggered by trust. I saw Jane in love, romantically, but awkwardly so; and regarded with a little more compassion my own first awkward attempts to love Mary, my wife. I saw Jane's tragic destiny and wished to possess her courage. I saw the moment of compassion and even understanding that passed between Jane and Feckenham at the end — an exchange I believe may actually have happened, on the grounds of something she said at the end of her interrogation. Through that moment I envisioned the possibility of reconciliation with my churchly enemies, the bishops and others who rejected so utterly my evangelical approach hooked as it was to an over-educated *curriculum vitae*. I wanted Dr. Feckenham to like me! I also wanted him to allow me to disagree with him.

So Jane Grey has been in my soul for sixteen years. It was through Jane that I discovered Katharine Parr, Jane's real mother in Christianity. It was through Katharine that I learned of Anne Askew, and then of Catherine Willoughby, who led me straight to Anne Bradstreet, and finally to Anne Boleyn. A Jungian analyst will observe immediately that Jane has become symbolic of my *anima*, although I am not a Jungian myself. Whatever Jane is for me, it is the true ground of my interest. And she has led me back and forth across and through the texts. Jane's story, in brief, I now present.

JANE was born in 1527. Her grandmother was the sister of Henry VIII. Jane's father was Henry Grey, the duke of Suffolk, and her mother Frances Brandon, daughter of the earlier duke of Suffolk, Charles Brandon. Jane's father was a committed, well-grounded Protestant of the earlier generation. Her mother was the wicked stepmother from any number of fairytales: one of the most appalling operators of any generation or class. Jane had two sisters. Her *two* tutors as a child were Mr. Harding, who later recanted his religion and became a Roman Catholic, and Mr. Aylmer, who fled to the continent under Mary and was appointed Bishop of London in 1576. Jane was fluent in French, Italian, Latin, and Greek, and could also read Hebrew. She really was a prodigy, no exaggeration.

But the emotional side of Jane's brilliance is also arresting. She comes into history with a reminiscence from Roger Ascham, who called on her father at Bradgate in April 1550. While awaiting the duke's return from stag hunting, Ascham came upon Jane reading a book, the *Phaedo* of Plato, in Greek, in a part of the house, now ruined, called ever after — or at least from the early 1800s on! — "Lady Jane's Tower." In Ascham's book *The Schoolmaster*, he recalls what Jane, who was about fourteen, said when he asked her why she was reading Plato for pleasure. He used her words to illustrate in his work how it is that a good teacher, in Jane's case John Aylmer, can compensate for hard and critical parents. Jane's reply to Ascham's question is worth quoting in full:

> I will tell you, and I will tell you a truth, which perchance you will marvel at. One of the greatest benefits which ever God gave me is, that he sent me such sharp and severe parents, and so gentle a schoolmaster. For when I am in the presence either of father or mother, whether I speak, keep silence, sit, stand, or go, eat, drink, be merry or sad; be sewing, playing, dancing, or doing any thing else, I must do it, as it were, in such weight, measure, and number, even so per-

fectly as God made the world, or else I am so sharply taunted, so cruelly threatened, yea, presently sometimes with pinches, nips, and bobs, and other ways which I will not name for the honour I bear them, so without measure misordered, that I think myself in hell, till time come that I must go to Mr. Aylmer, who teaches me so gently, so pleasantly, with such fair allurements to learning, that I think all the time nothing [i.e., time flies] while I am with him; and when I am called from him, I fall to weeping, because whatsoever I do else but learning, is full of grief, trouble, fear, and wholly misliking unto me. And thus my book has been so much my pleasure, and brings daily to me more and more pleasure; in respect of it all other pleasures in very deed are but trifles and troubles unto me.[1]

How can anyone read Jane's words without being moved? Today we would tend to say that she was an abused child who found refuge in her head. But you can feel the emotion, the self-knowledge, the astonishing articulateness for a young teenager who would, in our milieu, be part of the junior-high youth group! Jane's fire, her self-understanding, her unconditionally weak situation in the face of awesome endowed gifts makes her reply to Roger Ascham one for the ages. Engravings of her conversation with Ascham were popular in England in the nineteenth century. I own one!

Two letters of Jane to Heinrich Bullinger, the Reformer of Zürich, who succeeded Ulrich Zwingli after Zwingli was killed at the Second Battle of Kappel, have survived. Jane's first letter thanks Bullinger for his advice concerning the best way for her to master

---

1. Roger Ascham, *The Schoolmaster* (1570), ed. Lawrence V. Ryan, Folger Documents of Tudor and Stuart Civilization 13 (Charlottesville: The University Press of Virginia, 1967), 35-36.

Hebrew. The second letter thanks him for taking the time to take her theological questions seriously. Bullinger's letters to Jane have not survived. For Jane at age fifteen to have written letters of inquiry to one of the most famous scholars in Europe, a man whose Reforming work she wholly admired, is simply amazing.

IN 1553, as King Edward, the sincerely Protestant king, Henry VIII's son, began to sicken, a shadow came over Jane's life. The shadow finally darkened her way completely, and snuffed out her light. It happened as follows.

John Dudley, the duke of Northumberland and the key "handler" of King Edward, saw an unstoppable train bearing down on England: the accession of Mary Tudor, a Catholic, to the throne. As Edward's half-sister, Henry's daughter by Katherine of Aragon, she was the legal heir if Edward should die. But because Jane had a direct blood link to the throne, a case could be made that Jane was next in the line of succession, but only if Mary Tudor were disallowed. So Northumberland sought to change the act of succession. Dudley played on Edward's extremely conscientious Protestantism, especially vulnerable in his extremity of sickness. Edward actually signed a change in the act of succession naming Jane as his heir. At the same time, or rather just before the signing, John Dudley got Jane's father and mother to force Jane to marry his own son Guilford. Guilford Dudley is usually depicted as a cipher, a sort of naive and gangly, duped youth, painfully the inferior to Jane in every way. No one really knows enough about Guilford to say. At any rate, Jane was forced into marrying him, and the wedding took place at the end of May 1553.

Edward died on July 6. Northumberland did obeisance to Jane on July 10, and she was queen!: The Nine Days Queen.

Having been forced into it, Queen Jane was now the creation, after the fact, of her implacable handlers. She was caught between three inexorable forces: John Dudley, for whom she was the totem of his own ambition to remain in power; her mother and now also her father the duke of Suffolk, who raised a (meagre) army to defend her; and the Princess Mary Tudor, who was able to escape from Framlingham Castle in Suffolk and to whom supporters, not exclusively Catholics, began to rally. Everyone seemed to understand that Dudley had forced Jane's claim and that it was simply unbinding as long as the regular heir, Mary, were alive. Most Protestants had enough horror of meddling in the divine right of royal blood that they conceded the justice of Mary's claim.

Jane's role in the cooked-up coup of her new father-in-law, John Dudley, Guilford's father, might have been forgiven if her own natural father, Henry Grey, had not now taken up arms against Mary. And Mary herself would have found it hard to clear Jane in any case because of Jane's intense and articulate commitment to the Reformed Religion. That commitment was no secret.

John Foxe relates two anecdotes of how Jane fell foul of Mary over religion. The first incident was witnessed and is almost certainly true.

> During [her] visit [to the Lady Mary at Newhall], [Jane's] piety and zeal against popery, prompted her to reprove the Lady Ann Wharton, for making a courtesy to the host, or consecrated wafer, enclosed in a box, suspended, as was then usual, over the altar. Lady Jane observing her companion courtesy, asked if the princess were coming. Her companion replied No, but she made obeisance to Him that made us all. Why, said Lady Jane, how can that be he that made us all, for the baker made him? which being carried by some officious person to the ear of the princess, was retained in her heart, so that she never loved Lady Jane afterwards.[2]

---

2. As quoted in *The Precious Remains of the Lady Jane Grey* (London: The Religious Tract Society, 1831), 6.

Simple common sense encounters the reserved sacrament! Was Jane guilty of "objectifying" or overly concrete thinking? Or was she interpreting Scripture?

On another occasion Jane was given some gold and valuable cloth as a present from Mary. Jane asked, "What shall I do with it?" "Wear it," said a lady-in-waiting. "Nay," answered Jane, "It would be a shame to follow my lady Mary against God's Word, and leave my lady Elizabeth who followeth God's word." Jane's reply implied a nascent Puritan allergy to finery and outward signs of personal vanity, but was, of course, an extremely incautious thing to say.

When the duke of Northumberland's pathetic little standing army, mustered up to defend Queen Jane, fled overnight, and when Henry Grey's expeditionary force also melted away, the whole country, the Protestants reluctantly, agreed that Mary was the legal queen. A mere fourteen days, in fact, from Northumberland's obeisance, Jane's reign was ended and she became a prisoner in the Tower of London.

What were Jane's thoughts when the world crashed down around and upon her? She is reported to have said, "I now willingly . . . relinquish the crown, and endeavor to salve those faults committed by others, if at least so great a fault can be salved, by a willing relinquishment and ingenuous acknowledgment of them." A letter is also preserved from August 1553 in which she apologized in detail for acceding to Northumberland's wishes, and the wishes of her parents in accepting the crown. This letter may not be genuine.

The one statement we know she made is from the morning of her execution, February 12. This statement reflects her true mind concerning the political aspects of her actions: "The act against the queen's highness was unlawful, and the consenting thereunto by me; but touching the procurement and desire thereof by me, or on my behalf, I do wash my hands thereof in innocency before God, and the face of you good christian people this day." In short, Jane knew she had been used, and, in acknowledging her wrong in succeeding to pressure (it was the story of her life), she affirmed that it was not her idea.

Jane and Guilford were both condemned to die for treason. They both held out hope for a pardon, as they were even in that day and age regarded as young offenders. Everyone knew, as well, that John Dudley was the true culprit. But a pardon could never really come, for Jane's existence would always be regarded as a magnet for rebellion under Mary. For similar reasons of state, Mary Queen of Scots would "have" to die during the reign of Queen Elizabeth.

Jane was examined on the eleventh of February by John Feckenham, Queen Mary's chaplain, in hopes of securing her recantation of the Reformed Religion and her return to Rome. That examination was Jane's finest hour. The written record of it is the best source for her theological opinions. Jane also wrote a letter to her father, dated February 9; a long letter to her former tutor Harding, who had returned to Catholicism; a note to her sister Catherine on the flyleaf of her New Testament; and also a prayer that has come down to us from her time of imprisonment.

Guilford was beheaded the morning of February 12. It is reported, probably correctly, that Jane was overcome with emotion when she saw the cart carrying his head and body wheeled through the courtyard below her cell or chamber. Guilford died a Protestant.

Jane herself died with great courage. Her speech was short. She even witnessed to the Reformed Religion in a subtle but explicit manner, calling on the crowd to "assist me with your prayers, *while I am alive.*" She meant by this that she rejected prayers for the dead and saw this present life as the decisive arena for the certainty of her salvation. Her inexperience and youth came out only in her repeated, moving questions to the executioners and to her ladies, "What shall I do?" "Where is the block?" "Where is it?"

Jane was called upon, really from the day she was born, to act above her age. Her cry, "What shall I do?" lingers in the memory among other remembered incidents concerning her. It is a cry that is burned into my consciousness. Jane evokes a searing sympathy.

DID Jane fall in love with Guilford? Was she given consolation, comfort, and human affection from any one at any time? It is not possible to say. She certainly responded to Feckenham, for although she stood him up theologically, she thanked him at the scaffold for his humanity to her. "God will abundantly requite your goodness." Jane surely also loved her Dr. Aylmer.

In the nineteenth century, the box that enclosed Jane's skull in the Church of St. Peter at Vincula by the Tower of London was opened by some antiquarians. The skull had disintegrated into dust. Jane's theology, however, remains a crag and a rock.

There was another legacy, however, a legacy of which Jane herself would have been uniquely proud. It was the manner of her own father's death. He kept the faith: Jane's Protestant faith.

Here is Henry Grey's short speech, delivered eleven days after his daughter's execution at the same spot. Henry Grey's speech was more of a theological testament than Jane's, and was preceded by an almost comic exchange between the duke and another of the queen's hot Catholic chaplains, Dr. Weston. The duke persisted — at such a time! — in refusing to allow Weston to mount the platform with him. Weston persisted, in return. On the third try, Weston gave up and held back.

Henry Grey addressed these words to the crowd: "Masters, I have offended the queen, and her laws, and thereby am justly condemned to die, and am willing to die, desiring all men to be obedient; and I pray God that this my death may be an example to all men, beseeching you all to bear me witness, that I die in the faith of Christ, trusting to be saved by his blood only (and not by any trumpery), the which died for me, and for all of them that truly repent, and steadfastly trust in him."

"Saved by his blood only (and not by any trumpery)"! This is the living, dying testament of Jane's father, a resisting Reformer, keeping faith with his daughter so traduced, holding the faith militantly even at the end. As Holinshed, William Shakespeare's historian, wrote: "Such was the end of this duke of Suffolk. . . . He was a hearty friend unto the gospel, and professed it to the last."

THE TEXTS

Jane's letters to Heinrich Bullinger, preserved in the City Library at Zürich; her letters at the end to her father, to her sister Catherine, and to her tutor, Dr. Harding; her prayer book and New Testament; and a prayer we have from her: these comprise her precious remains. The letter to Dr. Harding, written in the Tower, is a scorcher, possibly her sharpest blast, a passionate outburst against the Whore of Rome.[3]

All of these are preserved. Given her young age, and also in the context of her execution as a traitor, it is a miracle that so much is left. Going through her letters and the anecdotes here and there that are well attested allows entry to her story. But it is small entry. Walking through Bradgate Park today and surveying the remains of the brick house in which she lived and for which "stark" is the only adjective, then taking in further the ancient pollarded oaks along the road to the house — oaks that look like the inhabited

---

3. Jane apparently also left behind three aphorisms, composed the night of February 11 in the Tower. They are as follows: "If justice is done with my body, my soul will find mercy with God" (composed in Latin); "Death will give pain to my body for its sins, but the soul will be justified before God" (composed in Greek); "If my faults deserve punishment, my youth at least, and my imprudence were worthy of excuse; God and posterity will show me favor" (composed in English).

horrible ones in *Snow White:* making such a pilgrimage is to be a part of one of history's tragedies. It is the story of "one untimely born," whose little body bore the crushing weight of politics: the wrong time, the "wrong" religion, the wrong parents, the "wrong" husband, the "wrong" birth, the "wrong" past, the "wrong" present, and an unjustified niche in history's future.

Yet the texts tell us much — especially that Jane was a zealot, despite all the choking circumstances snuffing her out; that her conversations were incapable of being smothered; that she was gripped by something beyond herself. How can one explain her grace under pressure in the face of Feckenham's probing? How touching it is also that she was grateful to Feckenham, that she thanked him for his kindness at the end, and that she begged him to change his mind about the Gospel for *his* soul's sake.

Feckenham's interview with Jane is the locus for this consideration of Jane's theology. It was a public disputation and took place in the chapel of the Tower of London, probably on February 11, either two days or possibly one day before Jane's death. It was probably also recorded by a stenographer. The interview reveals both Jane Grey and John Feckenham at the height of their powers, although Feckenham was at least twenty years older than Jane.

HER THEOLOGY

Feckenham was the examiner and Jane the examined. As in almost all Reformation-era disputes, the disputants acknowledged from the start that nothing separated them with regard to the Trinity and with regard to the two great commandments of the Law. Jane, however, declares that faith alone — i.e., trust in God — justifies the human being; Feckenham wants her to say that the works of the Law also justify. This Jane denies.

Then comes the question that was for Jane and her generation of Reformers the decisive one: What is a sacrament? Jane declares that there are but two sacraments, versus the church's seven. She invokes the New Testament to back two, not seven, but Feckenham does not yet wish to get into the question of authority, i.e., Scripture versus church: "Well, we will talk of that herewith," he says.

Concerning the Eucharist, Jane states that the bread and the wine signify the body and the blood. She sees Christ's words as figures of speech. She denies that Christ's body (i.e., his human nature) can be ubiquitous. The natural or corporeal body of Christ can exist in one place only at one time: "God forbid that I should say that I eat the very natural body and blood of Christ; for then either I should pluck away my redemption, *or else there were two bodies or two Christs* or twelve bodies, when his disciples did eat his body, and it suffered not till the next day" (my emphasis).

Jane is consistent in distinguishing, as a theologian should, between different levels of signification and different meanings of the same word. She understands that the church's literal (if faithful) interpretation of "This is my body" is empirically invalid as well as unsubtle, as in "It all depends on what 'is' is" (Bill Clinton).

Feckenham now goes to the authority question. He taxes Jane with believing Protestant interpreters before believing the church. Jane answers this one squarely. "No, I ground my faith upon God's word, and not upon the church." She also leaps back a century and takes up the charge of John Hus, that Rome denies the laity one half of the sacrament: "But surely I think if they deny it to us, then deny they to us part of our salvation. Moreover, I say, that it is an evil church, and not the spouse of Christ, but the spouse of the devil, that alters the Lord's supper. . . . To that church, say I, God will add plagues, and from that church will he take their part out of the book of life." Jane is in full sail, better, under full steam, ready for Dr. Harding in her mind, as Feckenham himself was a kinder, nicer man.

Feckenham then gave up and said that "he was sorry for her; for I am sure, quoth he, that we two shall never meet [again]."

Now Jane concludes her public theological life with a truly awesome clap of thunder. "True it is that we shall never meet [again], except God turn your heart; for I am assured unless you repent, and turn to God, you are in an evil case; and I pray God, in the bowels of his mercy, to send you his Holy Spirit, for he hath given you his great gift of utterance, if it pleases him also to open the eyes of your heart."

Jane's authority to speak as she does in a public academic debate at the age of sixteen, the day or two before her certain execution, has got to be one of the *momenta mirabila* in the history of early modern England. You have to stand amazed!

To sum up the theology of Jane Grey: She believed in justification by grace through faith, the root of love consisting in faith and not the other way around. She was a "Lutheran" in soteriology. She was a "Zwinglian" or symbolist/memorialist in her theology of the two sacraments. She took what we now tend to call "Calvin's" view of the heavenly session of Christ's human nature, ruling out his physical presence in the elements of the communion. She placed Scripture over church and shared on the question of authority the views of Luther, Calvin, and Zwingli. The fact that the largest section by far of the debate with Feckenham is given over to the question of Christ's presence in the Eucharist makes it clear that Jane is part of the second generation of Reforming thought, for whom the Mass or Lord's Supper had become the apple of discord. Had Jane survived, I believe her attention would have moved along, as it did for Catherine Willoughby, to the question of election and the eternally benign inscrutability of the *deus absconditus* or hidden God.

Jane Grey

INTERPRETATION

"Under my Thumb" is an old Rolling Stones song about the triumph of power in the male-female arena. The sentiment has worked eternally both ways, both male over female and female over male. But Jane Grey is certainly the presenting case in this study of the unhappy straitened child under the thumb of mother and father; of John Dudley (not his son Guilford); then of her cousin Mary as queen; and finally, because of Mary's power, under the thumb of John Feckenham. Feckenham, by the way, was the mildest of them all.[4]

In other words, Jane Grey lived in a world of powermongering, but had no power herself. She was *forced* to retreat to the world of books and ideas. She was *forced* to marry a man she had never met by his father, who saw Jane solely as a means to an end. She was *forced* to take the crown despite her magnified protests against it. She was *forced* to defend the Reformed Religion — or recant! — within a situation in which her life depended on it. She was *forced* to give up her life at the age of sixteen. The closest that you and I get to a teenage death is at funerals caused by a drug overdose, or a suicide following a romantic rejection, or a Friday night car crash.

Yet "Victory is mine, saith the Lord." Jane became the spiritual prodigy of her age. She strengthened her husband so that he did

---

4. His mild tenor becomes apparent in the record of his own interrogations from the (Protestant) Bishop of Ely much later, during the reign of Elizabeth. Feckenham had to spend years and years as a prisoner-at-ease in the Tower of London because he would not conform to Elizabeth's Reformation settlement. She got some of her best bishops to try to persuade him to come over (i.e., from Rome), but he would not. But his arguments and also his confessions are not those of a fanatic. In other words, Jane was tougher, clearer, more uncompromising than Feckenham. It is hard to imagine Jane Grey as a middle-aged adult. In the times in which she lived, she was almost bound to go out in a blaze, either of glory or of ignominy.

not recant, and not the other way round. She had the last word on John Dudley, for when *he* recanted to Roman Catholicism before his own death, she told her warders that she had always known he was insincere. She "misliked" her nine-day crown and would not permit Guilford to call himself "king." Jane gave better than she took in the disputation with Feckenham and forced him to retire without the slightest hope of success. Her speech at the end said it all exactly right.

At age sixteen Jane was a daughter, not a mother; a princess, not a queen; a student, not a teacher. In fact, in crisis, she became the queen to many subjects, and the teacher to her teachers. Her own nemesis was undoubtedly her mother, and it was her mother who landed well, after the beheading of both husband and daughter. It was her mother who caused opprobrious scandal soon after these events by marrying a twenty-one-year-old stable groom. Her mother is the Wicked Witch of the West in this story, as unprincipled as her daughter had been principled.

But Jane also became mother to her father. Her father, the duke of Suffolk, Henry Grey, comes across very well at the end of the tale. He sought to keep faith with his daughter by rallying his servants to free her and vindicate her. They both went to their deaths knowing that she probably would have survived had not he and his men shouted for "Queen Jane." Yet he died in the Protestant faith, and his touching, rather "male" efforts to face death without a priest move the reader today. His witness to the sole-atoning death of Christ, with "no trumpery," is marvelous. Jane could not have hoped for better. Henry Grey's child had become the mother to her father.

A FINAL word of interpretation on Jane relates to her literal and "either-or" thinking. If there is a refrain among Jane's objections to the Roman doctrine, it is this: "Was Christ a door? Was he a vine?" She is at pains to criticize the use of "is" in the expression, "This is my body." Christ cannot have meant this, Jane states, because he elsewhere speaks symbolically and metaphorically of himself, rather than concretely or objectively. In sacramental theology, Jane was a symbolist.

Does this mean she was unsubtle?, thinking childishly, unable to grasp that "is" carries meaning on more than one level?, that the bread could be his body but on a level deeper than the seen and a level higher than the visible? Was her concrete concept of the received Roman doctrine unsubtle? Or was it a breath of fresh air that the stupefied world of the medieval church was needing to hear? Was Jane an adolescent thinker, unable to see what an adult should be able to see? Or was she the essential child who says, "Look everyone! The emperor has no clothes."

I myself discover Jane as the latter, the "child" wise-man who sees the obvious truth that no one else will see. When she would not curtsy before the host in Mary Tudor's chapel, she was declaring the obvious, prophetically even, if injudiciously, from a worldly point of view. "The Lord God dwelleth not in temples made with hands" (Acts 7:48). Jane was entirely synchronous on this score with Anne Askew. She was the critic we all need to know in order to pierce the veil of delusion and deception.

Jane's "enthusiasm" regarding the emperor that has no clothes is depicted vividly in the first scene after the credits in the very fine 1985 *Lady Jane*. Played by Helena Bonham Carter, Jane lays out Feckenham, played by Michael Hordern, when she states that it is superstition to believe that the bread of the mass can become the Lord's body. She takes a piece of bread and eats it, right up in the man's face, as if to say, "See . . . !"

There is a mischievous side to the Protestant impulse, a little bit of Toto, who brings down the curtain of deceit which hides the (very human) Wizard of Oz at the end of that particular classic. But just as Frank Baum "resurrects" the real power of the Wizard in the Wizard's act of imputing counterintuitive gifts to the cowardly lion, the tin woodsman, and the scarecrow, so Jane helps us to recover the real impact of the Gospel. Jane places belovedness before the works of love and thus sets the mainspring of human creativity and compassion within the prior creative love that comes from God. Jane's youthful, puckish rebellious streak serves to give us now a golden view into the one thing which counts, the divine Trust to us which engenders our trust in Him.

Chapter Five

CATHERINE WILLOUGHBY

(1520-1580)

Catherine Willoughby became the duchess of Suffolk in 1533 and was related directly to Lady Jane Grey. Catherine, like Jane, was a "royal" by blood. She was also ubiquitous in court circles and more importantly, both to her and to this book, was ubiquitous in Reforming circles. Everywhere we turn in the later reign of Henry VIII, Catherine is found among the Bible-reading fellowship closeted at court. She was one of Katharine Parr's inner circle, studied Scripture at the side of Anne Askew, and watched as nine-year-old prodigy Jane Grey became an unquenchable spokesman for the movement by her mid-teens.

Of the first generation of Reformation women, none but Catherine Willoughby (and Elizabeth Tudor), lived past her thirty-fifth birthday. Her story, like the others', is both noble and tragic. Catherine's particular cross was that she lived into late middle age. Eric Erikson said that religious reformers need to die young! Who can imagine an elderly Jesus?

Catherine's hour of glory came during her incredible adventures in Holland, Germany, Poland, and Lithuania, to which she fled to escape the agents of Mary. Looking back now, the years that followed were an anticlimax. Peaceful existence as a frustrated Puritan — which is what she really was — under Queen Elizabeth could not fulfill her sharp assertive gifts. Her older age was sad.

Catherine Willoughby's life and surviving texts, all letters, make us reflect on Christianity in its relation to the integration of personality; Christianity and the raising of adult unhappy children (and their mates), and Christianity and anxiety — for Catherine became anxious and peevish at the end of her life. Her final letters are discouraging, in fact, for they testify against her as to the consoling, strengthening character of faith. Something went wrong, and a theological issue lies probably at the root.

HER LIFE IN BRIEF

The backgrounds of celebrated characters are never scrutinized until they enter the public eye. Little is known, therefore, about Catherine Willoughby's early life. It was not until September 1533, when she married her guardian, Charles Brandon, the duke of Suffolk, that she emerged into the light of history. She was thirteen, and he was forty-eight. They were to have two children, Henry Brandon and Charles Brandon.

The great question concerning Catherine's early life is this: How was she converted to the New Religion? Jane Grey had grown up in it, and the unmediated presence of God the Father must surely have meant the difference to her between survival and complete suppression and eclipse. Jane said exactly that to Roger Ascham at Bradgate.

But what about Anne Boleyn, and Anne Askew, and Katharine Parr? How did they first find Christ in the new way? And now Catherine Willoughby? It is simply not known what inward springs and development turned these brilliant women into unquenchable, irrefutable adherents of the Protestant faith.

It is a little easier to trace the spiritual progress of Jeanne d'Albret, Queen of Navarre and their contemporary in France, who carried forward the same convictions, usually called "Calvinist," under comparable pressures across the English Channel. There are simply more documents extant from Jeanne d'Albret and her early development. Even with Jeanne, however, the inner or psychological changes are hard to detect.

It was easier, from the standpoint of human development, for Jane Grey to hold the line under threat, excommunication, and the fear of imminent death, for *Jane had never not been a part of the Reformed Church.* But Anne and Anne, Katharine and Catherine were all born into Catholicism. Other Reformation spirits, like Harding and John Dudley, went back to their roots, returning to Catholicism when the world came strong against them. John Dudley's wife also returned to Catholicism before she died, as did Jane Grey's mother. And not entirely from "trimming," for once their husbands were dead, no one really cared whether they attended mass or not.

So why did our older four stand and not retreat? Why did they stay with the change until death? What we do know is that in Catherine Willoughby's case, she ventured everything on her religion and took extreme risks to stay the course. And when she returned to England in better times, she kept at the cause, becoming a dinosaur of the Reform, whose long and studded tail twitched and banged until she was heard, and heard again.

What I think we can say regarding the steel of our heroes' convictions is that in each case their new convictions were made firmer by means of affliction, loss, and harassment. Anne Boleyn had to grow up overnight as she became the lightning rod to every religious trend, Protestant as well as Catholic, in a nation for which Christianity was the issue of life. Anne Askew fled her husband from Lincoln down to London, and something of that necessary move towards self-expression and autonomy involved a "leaving all" for the following of the Lord. Katharine Parr, too, was blistered in the oven of Gardner's threats. She found herself in a do-or-die situation.

It seems that most of the Reforming spirits of the age traveled through some fiery furnace of their own before arriving at the quality of conviction which steeled them to withstand persecution. You can see this steel tempered by fire if you make a study of the portraits-from-life of these people, several of which survive today. Years ago I noticed a quality of absolute tenacity in the picture of Théodore de Bèze that hangs at the Bibliothèque du Protestantisme at Paris. The same eyes peer out at you from the portrait of Gaspard de Coligny, Admiral of France and murdered marshall of the Huguenots. It is the same with the portrait of William the Silent of the Netherlands and with Henri de Rohan, the last, defeated preacher and general of the French Protestants. You see it also in the wonderful drawing from the life of Philippe du Plessis-Mornay, the Reformed apologist and political scientist. And you see it in the miniature of Catherine Willoughby herself, an exquisite likeness from the life, which survives at Grimsthorpe Castle.

Each of these was a Calvinist in the proper sense of the word. Each passed through a pall of defeat or near-death illness or winnowing loss. Ulrich Zwingli himself, who mentored Bullinger, Jane Grey's famous correspondent, is the prototype, for he "leapt like a calf from the stall" (Malachi 4:2) only after he had just barely survived the plague. Zwingli got the plague, strangely survived it, and therefore ever after had nothing left to lose.

AND Catherine Willoughby? What was her catharsis in the convictions to which she had evidently already come? It was the death of her two sons in the summer of 1551. Catherine's sons, Henry and Charles Brandon, were students at St. John's College when the "sweating sickness" seized Cambridge. No one has ever been able to explain to me exactly what this disease was. English medicine possessed no insight at that time into its origin or nature. It struck old and young as an extremely rapid, lethal fever which, once it infected you, caused death within a few hours. Although Henry and Charles had left Cambridge to escape it, it caught them at their mother's rented house at Buckden, outside the city. Henry died before his mother could get there. By the time Catherine had arrived, Charles had fallen unconscious. Their sudden deaths essentially dropped from out of a clear blue sky.

A widow, highly unpopular already with roughly half of the governing elite of her country, Catherine was taken completely off guard by the loss of her children. It is a wonder that she recovered at all.

A window into her faith, as the elixir that held her entire personality and psycho-genetic system together, is found in the letter she composed to her friend William Cecil, later Lord Burleigh, about one month after her loss. Cecil, who, you remember, was Katharine Parr's supporter, also became Catherine Willoughby's sole refuge and source of hope in her later years. This is what Catherine Willoughby wrote to William Cecil:

I give God thanks, good Master Cecil, for all His benefits which it hath pleased him to heap upon me; and truly I take this last (and to the first sight most sharp and bitter) punishment not for the least of His benefits, inasmuch as I have never been so well taught by any other before to know His power, His love and mercy, mine own weakness and that wretched state that without Him I should endure here. And to ascertain you that I have received great comfort in Him, I would gladly do it by talk and sight of you. But as I must confess myself no better than flesh, so I am not well able with quiet to behold my very friends without some part of these vile dregs of Adam to seem sorry for that whereof I know I rather ought to rejoice.

This excerpt is a window into the very least of Catherine's biographers. She calls Cecil "good," which is rare usage for her and suggests feeling. She uses the verb "heap" for God's gifts and benefits. A psychological writer would say she felt "heaped upon." I am sure she did. She acknowledges her wound to be "sharp and bitter," and also unique (i.e., "I have never been so well taught"). She understood her state "here" to be wretched. She says that she would like to *see* Cecil, and his wife Mildred, whom she loved. She would wish to speak with him in the flesh, but fears she will break down in their presence. She fears that her human nature, as a mourning mother, will take away her "quiet." And she understands her humanity to be "these vile dregs of Adam." She is obviously convincing herself of comfort.

Is there anything wrong with that? Clearly Catherine knows her feelings. She is as feeling in this letter as she is in others, for example the one where she laments Elizabeth's foot-dragging in the Reformation of the Church, and the several where she pleads for her grown children much later in her life. Catherine is engaged with God, with His strengthening purpose behind His depleting decrees. This is a powerful, conscious, and thus quite integrated statement of grief, all interpreted as best she is able in the context of the merciful God, and also presented horizontally. It is presented, that is, in the face of the Cecils' friendship and care for her. May all the mourning women and men of the world self-diagnose ourselves and so be enabled to converse with the Final Power that exists behind the thick curtain of ultimate meanings.

A COMFORT, an important comfort, came to Catherine within two years after her sons' deaths: she fell in love with and married Sir Richard Bertie. When her husband had died, the title Duke of Suffolk had reverted to Henry Grey, the father of Lady Jane. In the small world of the Tudor noble families, that title was conferred during the same ceremony at which John Dudley became duke of

Northumberland and William Cecil was knighted. Such a world was the inside of the Tudor power elite, ephemeral as their day in the sun was, save Cecil's.

No longer saddled with a titled "major player" as her husband, Catherine was free to do what she wished. It is typical that the heroines of this study always ached to become private citizens. Thus Katharine Parr married Thomas Seymour weeks after Henry's death. Now Catherine Willoughby trusted Richard Bertie because he was her "gentleman usher." That meant that he was her escort at all official functions of the court, as well as a sort of factotum at Grimsthorpe. Bertie was also a committed Protestant. Hugh Latimer, Catherine's friend and confidant, and also *the* preacher of the Reformation in England, approved of the marriage and almost certainly solemnized it. Richard Bertie, who became the father of two children to Catherine, Susan and Peregrine, was Catherine's true life partner, unconditionally devoted to her welfare and protection, and, when the roof fell in, stalwart to the highest point of sacrifice.

When Mary Tudor entered London as queen on August 3, 1553, Catherine Willoughby, together with her husband Richard, knew they were a marked pair. Years before, Catherine had offended Stephen Gardiner, now become Mary's Lord Chancellor, by confessing in public her dislike of him. Gardiner now moved rapidly. The pretext was a debt owed to Henry VIII by Catherine's former husband, the duke of Suffolk. But Gardiner added a key question when he interrogated Richard Bertie: "I pray you if I may ask the question of my lady your wife, is she now as ready to set up the mass as she was lately to pull it down? . . . I pray you, think you it possible to persuade her?"

The writing was on the wall. The decision was taken to leave, immediately. Between four and five o'clock the morning of New Year's Day, 1555, Catherine and a very small band of servants left their house in London, sailed down the river, met Richard, and sailed in the direction of the Netherlands. They were so afraid of being caught that they got lost in the fog. Every one of the servants missed the boat.

By the time they pushed off, it was down to Catherine, Richard, their tiny baby daughter Susan, and one good sailor. Once they had to turn back, and when they had finally crossed the Channel, they got lost again in a fog. Catherine was thirty-six and wholly unused to existing without servants. It is one of the celebrated annals of the Reformation, this peregrination (hence their son's name, "Peregrine" — the wanderer!), for they were truly without name or language or protection or friend. Their goal was the town of Wesel. There they hoped that an exiled English Protestant minister would receive them and shelter them.

The high point of this story is the arrival of Catherine, Richard, and baby Susan *tous seuls* in Wesel, where the inns were all full and, having nowhere to go, they took shelter, like the Holy Family, in the half-shelter of the porch of St. Willibrord's Church. At the end of his rope, Richard, who knew no Dutch and could communicate only in Latin, the *lingua franca* among educated people, of whom he seemed to meet very few in these circumstances, knocked on the door of the house next door to the church. He was prepared penniless to plead for shelter on his knees. But it was the English pastor's house! From that point, there was light, and hope. The Berties stayed with their coreligionists for several weeks, Catherine in fact became pregnant, and they went to church in the Protestant Reformed manner.

Fear of Gardiner's agents and Catholic informers, however, drove them on. Once again they moved, and traveled to Weinheim in Germany, where the duke was friendly to Protestantism. Even there, however, they were vulnerable, because it was an area of mixed religion. They were attacked at one point, in their little covered wagon which looked like a nineteenth-century American "prairie schooner." They were all almost killed by mercenary soldiers. Bertie distinguished himself in courage, resourcefulness, faithfulness, and faith.

The extraordinary thing is that they pressed on. Their goal became Poland. This was because Poland was now Protestant, a concept that today sounds unbelievable, but was true for decades. They made it all the way to Poland, somewhat under the conditions in which Brigham Young finally got to the Salt Lake. There, finally, in Poland, King Sigismund ratcheted the tale up one more notch. He needed a governor to administer Lithuania, the northern province of Poland on the Baltic. Moreover, he needed a Protestant governor. So he enlisted the Berties to be his "Joseph in Egypt": an English knight and marchioness consort exiled only to govern. It is an amazing denouement to their road less traveled. Thus Catherine and Richard, Susan and Peregrine, spent their last year in exile administering a state that is now regarded as the stronghold of Roman Catholicism among the Baltic republics. No wonder Catherine's high doctrine of providence only grew higher.

THE family returned to England in the late spring of 1559, six months after "Bloody Mary" died. Catherine's letter to Cecil dated March 4 is a classic, and reflects her true state of mind concerning the state of the Reformation in England at that early point in Elizabeth's reign. The letter is printed in Appendix E below.

The gist of the letter is that Catherine was alarmed to discover, as were almost all the returning Protestant exiles, that Elizabeth was taking it slow. The new queen was not moving nearly as rapidly in the interests of reforming the church as her best supporters wished. It was the story of her reign writ large, this feeling letter of Catherine to Lord Burleigh and to his wife Mildred. This was the sign standing sadly over the rest of Catherine's life: her insistent impatience with Elizabeth. Elizabeth disliked enthusiasts in religion and kept her own thoughts to herself; Catherine had put everything at risk for her faith and was not afraid to speak her mind:

this conflict is apparent in every painful encounter they had, right through to Catherine's death in 1580.

The last twenty years of Catherine's life were spent, so far as is known, in obsessing with her children's rights and the rights of their spouses. Catherine spun her wheels, pathetically as it seems, trying to get Elizabeth to declare Susan's husband, Reginald Grey, the earl of Kent. She also devoted years of letter writing and personal appointments to seeking the title "Lord Willoughby" for her husband Richard Bertie. She succeeded in the first suit and failed in the second.

Then in 1577, the Berties' son Peregrine, who Queen Elizabeth actually liked, married a woman named Mary Vere. The letters extant from this period are all rueful complaints to Cecil and also to the earl of Leicester concerning the cantankerous "harridan" her son had married. Catherine's conflicts with Mary Vere, and her rather frustrated, even reluctant attempts to see the situation in the providence of God, are all we know of Catherine just before she died. The reader of her letters is struck by an obsessive vein within them. Their wheedling tone sounds unworthy of the woman who crisscrossed Europe under violent persecution without losing her nerve. After Catherine died on September 19, 1580, we know that both Susan's marriage and Peregrine's marriage produced grandchildren, and that both of Catherine's children came to later life happy and fulfilled.

THE TEXTS

The only texts from Catherine's own hand are her letters. Most important for the understanding of her theology are these: her letter to William Cecil, dated July 7, 1551, in the immediate aftermath of her sons' death; her letter to William and Mildred Cecil, dated March 4, 1559, concerning the state of the Reformation in England as Catherine returned from exile; and her letter, dated Easter Monday 1580, concerning Peregrine's unhappy, alienating marriage.

Other texts illuminating Catherine's life are the household receipts and records from Grimsthorpe Castle, where she ran the estate with her husband for many years. There are also Hugh Latimer's sermons on the Lord's Prayer, which were preached in Catherine's presence at Grimsthorpe during King Edward's reign. These sermons themselves are less useful than one might hope, for they are filled with fairly generic attacks on Rome and homespun anecdotes drawn mostly from agriculture and from trades like shoemaking, rather than theological argument. Latimer's sermons are worlds away from Anne Askew's or Jane Grey's interrogations, for they are neither closely reasoned nor intended to convince by logic. I will focus instead on Catherine's handwritten letters.

CATHERINE'S THEOLOGY

Catherine's personal theology, as I think we can term it, struggled with the themes that concerned the third phase of the Reformation in England. The first phase, evident in Anne Boleyn's and Katharine Parr's legacy, concerned the core issue of justification by grace through faith. The second phase, seen in Anne Askew's and Lady Jane Grey's literary remains, saw the Mass and the issue of the Eucharist as the main stage. The third phase, extending to the 1640s and through to the troubles that led to the Civil War, became entangled with the question of divine will, providence, and election, and, to a lesser extent, also with church government and the degree of Reformation change that was proper in respect to institutions.

Catherine Willoughby's theology was characterized by an extremely high doctrine of providence. This is unmistakable in her letter to the Burghleys after the death of her sons Charles and

Henry. She wishes to understand the crushing blow to her "flesh" (i.e., to her normal inescapable human feelings) as a mercy. She means that by taking away from her, her very most cherished prerogative — her children and her attachment to them — God has intentionally forced her to rely solely on Him. Catherine's reasoning is identical to Jane Grey's, when, at the beginning of her public examination by Feckenham, she states, "And as for my heavy case, I thank God I do so little lament it that rather I account the same for a more manifest declaration of God's favor toward me than ever he showed me any time before."

Talk about counterintuitive! But this is the high concept of God's absolutely good will for his children which flowed irresistibly out of Luther's equally absolutely high concept of God's grace. If grace alone saves, then God alone is the willing actor in all human events. Luther's concept of the electing God comes out loud and clear in *Bondage of the Will*. And the second generation, together with the entire third generation, of Protestant Reformers echoes the cry. God's providence is all. He alone has free will. He alone is capable of deciding anything. The slings and arrows of human experience come from God.

Contemporary people make heavy weather of this. Our ancestors generally accepted it. It is true in any event, and in all contexts of time and place, that the human being is not in control. Call it *karma* or the Higher Power or the Other or "what is written" or destiny or "this is what was meant to happen" or "everything has a reason": no human person confronted with the givens or limits of life can possibly assert that he or she is "free" in any uninhibited or unconditional sense of the word. In any event, Catherine Willoughby believed in God's will as her "personal trainer," in every detail, and most poignantly, in the blows rained on her by disease and exile (and later by in-laws!).

Catherine's second preoccupation in theology was the purity of the church. She said that Christ (alone) is head of the church, and that Christ's wish for his body, the church, is found alone in the Bible. She rejected confession and creed, as in her unexpected repudiation of the Augsburg Confession as a "work of man." She rejected the Roman yoke. She wanted a Bible-led and Bible-organized church and saw no mediating structure or authority between Bible-prototype and her own context. This has always been the cry of "renewal"-oriented Christians: no king but Christ, no head but Jesus', crowned with thorns. It is not anachronistic to understand Catherine as a Puritan. She anticipates the arguments of Walter Travers, Richard Hooker's Puritan opponent, and was out of step with the future, or at least the immediate future, as chartered and settled by Elizabeth. It is possible that Catherine and Richard Bertie were able to put their Puritan views of the church into practice in the village and estates they governed in Lincolnshire, though there is little or no direct evidence of that. But in every department, Catherine disapproved of caution and tempering — better, trimming — in the great matter of church Reformation. She was absolute, then, in her assertion of absolute divine providence, and was also absolute in her application of the written divine will to the human experience of church or *ecclesia*.

There is a third point to make concerning Catherine's theology. I think it was less "integrated" or whole than the theology of Anne Askew and Jane Grey. Anne Askew and Jane Grey died exactly as they had lived. Biographers have sought to make much of Jane's somewhat nicer words to Feckenham at the end of her examination. That may be — although the evidence is slight. But her speech at the scaffold, and her last written words to her sister, are bold as blazes!

Catherine Willoughby, however, unlike her sisters in Reform, lived to be an old woman, at least by sixteenth-century standards. Her letters at the end display a personality that is overcome by discouragement, by her frustration at Elizabeth's refusal to help her son-in-law receive his title and by Elizabeth's persistent refusal to grant one to Richard Bertie. Catherine is also sent "'round the bend" by her daughter-in-law Mary Vere.

In the last text we have from Catherine, she is even frustrated with God. How can the Lord of the absolutely good will be the one who frustrates her so, and Peregrine her son, by the invasive, witching attacks of Peregrine's wife, the alien in their house? Catherine's whining, and the complaint that she is stumped by the God whom she has served, suggest that she was unable to put together her faith and her experience. A critic might say, in the words of the bumper sticker seen on the cars of Americans who oppose the "religious right," "My karma ran over your dogma."

The point is that Catherine's theology sounds unintegrated, at least at the end. A vulnerability exists in her thought to the point of character defeat (her whining) and persistent frustration (her daughter-in-law). This is thoroughly human, yes, but also unsatisfying. Catherine's theology grew superficial towards the end, or, more precisely put, the existential stakes were lower, so that the original theology which had served her so well in the dark 1550s had shallower soil in which to bed. It is also possible to say that Catherine by nature was temperamentally afflicted with a certain narcissism, which gained in prominence the older she grew. Christian posterity can say, considering her witness: would that she had died younger!

INTERPRETATION

Rightly regarded as a Puritan, Catherine stands on the threshold of the advanced or "forward" zeal that would issue, on the right, in the high-church or "Laudian" reaction in the Church of England. The "Laudian" reaction (from Archbishop William Laud) to Tudor Protestantism and Puritans like Catherine Willoughby led to the violent explosions of the 1640s. It resulted finally in the Commonwealth of Oliver Cromwell. Catherine's forward Protestantism is seen in her testimony of acquiescence to the blows of God/fate/providence and in her forceful criticism of Elizabeth's snail's pace in the Reformation of the church. Her thinking puts her within the third generation of theologians, for whom both election and ecclesiology were the paramount issues.

Catherine's nemesis was Elizabeth. We know from several other cases that Elizabeth carried grudges, or held lasting bad opinions, against a person when there was one specific reason. Thus Archbishop Grindal was disgraced because of one letter he wrote. Jane Grey's sisters were put in jail because they married without consulting the queen. And the Lambeth Articles composed by Archbishop Whitgift were canceled simply because Whitgift had neglected to consult her.

What was the cause of Elizabeth's antipathy toward the Duchess of Suffolk? We will never know. What we do know is that had Catherine said the sky is blue, Elizabeth would have said, no it is red! Catherine could never get satisfaction from Elizabeth on any score in any circumstance. The queen's unquenchable animus toward Catherine has to exempt Elizabeth from the category of persons presented in this book. This is because had Elizabeth understood Reformation theology as the "one thing needful," as Boleyn, Askew, Parr, and Grey did, it would have softened her feelings about Catherine Willoughby's person. I am sure that theology came second to politics, and, to give her her due, to her "husband" England, within the conscious aims of Elizabeth. This was not so for Catherine Willoughby. Her flight to Germany demonstrates it. *Not* my country right or wrong.

The man who was the constant for Catherine throughout her whole life was William Cecil. They had a proven friendship which carries within itself an important book for someone to write, for there is no male-female "static" or mixed messages or psychosexual innuendo in any single sentence of their affecting correspondence. William and Mildred Cecil were the safe place for Catherine, notwithstanding her very important love, also, for Richard Bertie, who consecrated himself to her welfare for thirty years.

What we miss are Cecil's letters to Catherine! Did he ask her to temporize? Did he share her convictions? (We know he did essentially, from the introduction to Katharine Parr's book.) Did Cecil reason with her theologically, Christianly, when she fell apart at the end? Did he pray for her, did he feel with her when she crossed Europe as a refugee from Mary?

Catherine's story does not end with her tomb at Spilsby parish church, where she lies now beside her husband, their pitched labors over. It ends, within history "after the flesh," more likely in 1688 with the formal triumph of Protestantism in England.

For Americans, however, there is a further link of influence and interest. This is the link constituted by Anne Bradstreet. Anne grew up on Catherine's former estates at Tattershall, where her father was steward to the earl of Lincoln. The area was *impressed* with Puritanism, as the Berties had worked hard to win their servants, clients, and retainers to forward views. Exactly fifty years after Catherine died, whole Puritan communities left England and emigrated to New England. Anne Dudley Bradstreet and her husband Simon were no older than twenty when they sailed to Boston on the same ship, the *Arabella*, which also carried John Winthrop. Anne became America's first poet. It is not sentimental or farfetched to see Anne as Catherine Willoughby's direct successor, for Bradstreet's writings reflect the same great interests as Catherine's letters to Burghley. I think the Berties themselves would have emigrated to Massachusetts Bay Colony had they lived a half-century later than they did.

Among her poems, Anne Bradstreet wrote several short meditations on personal incidents involving death and loss, on the one hand, and recovery and gratitude, on the other. Here are some

verses Anne composed after a fire that destroyed the Bradstreets'
house at Andover, Massachusetts on July 10, 1666. They bear direct
comparison with Catherine Willoughby's letter composed in the
immediate aftermath of her sons' death from the sweating sickness
(see Appendix E).

In silent night when rest I took
For sorrow near I did not look
I wakened was with thund'ring noise
And piteous shrieks of dreadful voice.
That fearful sound of "Fire!" and "Fire!"
Let no man know is my desire.

I, starting up, the light did spy,
And to my God my heart did cry
To strengthen me in my distress
And not to leave me succorless.
Then, coming out, beheld a space
The flame consume my dwelling place.

And when I could no longer look,
I blest His name that gave and took,
That laid my good now in the dust.
Yea, so it was, and so 'twas just.
It was His own, it was not mine,
Far be it that I should repine . . . (ital. PZ)

Conclusion

The five theological women of this book comprise a mirror of the Protestant Reformation. Their "thinking together"[1] stands in almost exact parallel to the developments in theology that were taking place throughout Europe within the Reformation movement.

Thus, the books Anne Boleyn owned show that she was focused on justification by grace through faith and on the law-gospel antithesis. There is a high component of Luther's thought within Anne's remains, although it came by way of the "Lutherans" of France. Katharine Parr, too, in her piercing little book, *Lamentation of a Sinner,* presents a theology of justification in pure culture. The grace of God in Christ as prior to the works of love on our part in this world is Parr's deep resounding note in every sentence. I can

---

1. This phrase comes from the "crime" charged to the Kreisau Circle in Germany in 1945. The Kreisau Circle was a group of religious Protestant and Catholic Germans who resisted Hitler during the Second World War and were almost all executed by the Nazis in the aftermath of the July 20, 1944, attempt on the Führer's life. Helmuth James von Moltke, the coordinator of this band of Christian German intellectuals, said, just after the trial at which he was condemned to death, that the crime of the Kreisau Circle consisted in their having "thought together."

discover very little of the law, in the theological sense, in Parr's moving expression of personal, logical, humbled, cross-oriented theology.

In Anne Askew and Jane Grey, however, a new theme comes to the fore. This calls to mind Philipp Melanchthon's warning to Thomas Cranmer, that the Eucharist would become an apple of discord among the Reformers. In Askew's and Grey's case, it was the Eucharist not as inter-Protestant problem, but as *the* crucial point of opposition to the Church of Rome. Both women carried forward a particular argument. The ground of their argument was common sense. Obviously, they reasoned, Christ was not a door when he used that image of himself. Nor was he a gate. He spoke symbolically. Similarly, then, when he said that the bread of the Last Supper was his body, he meant it symbolically. He meant it non-objectively. Askew and Grey wanted to make a firm distinction between the thing (bread) and the thing signified (the body or presence of Christ).

We could say that these people were unsubtle, and that a symbol can, at different levels of meaning, operate as if it were the thing itself. But we can also approve the English Reformers' conscious lack of subtlety. They had had their fill of subtlety! The distinctions piled on distinctions that marked late medieval theories of the Mass were abstruse and fabulous. I believe Askew and Grey were right to declare that the emperor has no clothes. We should admire their common sense, courageously applied. We can say that their Christ was entirely larger than the Eucharist, possessed by no space and time, unmediated, spiritual in the sense of John 4:24, possessed therefore of all people. These women freed the presence of Christ's absence from an entirely artificial localization and did the world of practical theology a critically important service.

The third phase of Reformation theology is seen in the letters, and in the unhappiness, of Catherine Willoughby. Like Jane Grey in her counterintuitive understanding that her "heavy case" was the gift of God, Catherine Willoughby found impressive comfort in the "gift" of grief after her boys died. It was the providence of God to make her rely solely on his grace, which had taken Charles and Henry from her. And it was the enigma of providence that occupied John Calvin and his deep-thinking students at mid-century and later. It was the enigma of God's predestinating grace, as laid out by Luther in every one of its fundamentals in his *Bondage of the Will*, that occupied the Protestant world from late mid-century to the middle of the seventeenth century. Ironically, the doctrine was inadequate for Catherine at the end. It was inadequate in the context of her children's problems. Or, better, Catherine was unable to draw upon the providence of God in such a way that she could derive peace from it. Her conflict with providence probably says more about Catherine's temperament than it does about the weakness of the teaching she had received. We do not know enough to venture the percentages!

The overall point is that ideas, finally, drove these five women. Or, better, they themselves said that ideas drove them. It is well and good to say that men called the shots, for power politics did determine things, just as events and class drove the narratives of these people's lives. But they themselves were convinced that the witness they bore to Bible hopes and Bible diagnoses, together with the specific hand of God in all things, governed everything. Each one of the five women tells us through her texts that theology, Christ's mandates, the Word, was primary. Everything else was secondary. We have to accept this. If we fail to let the women speak — and they all spoke — we do them an injustice. They were theological activists and exponents. It is the most important thing about them.

But there is something else extremely important to add. Each of these women was especially vulnerable because she was a woman. Anne was at risk specifically because she was the "other woman" to Katherine of Aragon. Because of that fact, she could never be secure. Anne's insecurity was passed on to her daughter

Elizabeth. Katharine Parr was also the "other woman" but in a different sense. Her influence derived from her husband, and she also put on a mighty act when she realized she was in danger. Then, too, she proved vulnerable, or rather must have felt vulnerable, as she rushed to marry Thomas Seymour a month after Henry died. Katharine was definitely vulnerable to her gender and to her exposed position as Henry's queen, then as Henry's widow.

Anne Askew, the most mischievous and also the most physically heroic of the women, was also vulnerable because of her gender. It was not forgotten that she had left her husband. And she herself threw up to her examiners at every chance she had that she was "but a poor woman," "an ignorant woman," a "foolish woman." Jane Grey was vulnerable more because of her age than because of her sex. Even so, she was forced to marry Guilford Dudley and forced to let the crown be put on her head. I see Jane, however, more put upon because of her youth — like her cousin Edward, the boy-king, who was also a victim of politics and older, worldly men. Jane never talked of herself as a girl or woman, but only as a very young person compelled to swim deep waters.

Catherine Willoughby's exposure as a woman comes vividly in mind as we see her shivering in the church porch at Wesel, baby at the breast, no servants, her excellent husband going from inn to inn and door to door pleading for help. But again, Catherine's vulnerability has more to do with a certain quality of the "princess and the pea," a specific sort of complaining spirit born of privileged station, rather than with her being female. For the issue of gender is not always clear-cut at this time. The cause of Catherine's flight into exile was the power wielded by another woman, the Catholic Queen Mary, and Catherine's struggles with power in later life were, again, with another woman, Queen Elizabeth.

IN ADDITION, men often shared the same vulnerability as women. Anne Boleyn's brother was also executed and for the same charge.

John Bale, who had taken up Anne's case from exile in Basel, Switzerland, to which he had fled after the Roman Church drove him from the diocese in Ireland where he had been consecrated bishop, was also the captive of pirates for three years after he fled for refuge from Mary. Bale died exhausted and in terrible health because of the deprivations suffered on account of his Protestantism. Is he less of a victim than the woman he championed? Guilford Dudley, too: his head came off as surely as Jane's did, and at the same precise age; as did Jane's father, whom she strengthened to die with moving witness and light.

Then, too, Thomas Seymour, lost his head soon after the death of Katharine Parr. His deceptions and self-deceptions caught up with him.

Finally, there is Richard Bertie, who shared Catherine Willoughby's every loss and ate the bread of affliction with her for years and years. Having married her — the kiss of death from Queen Elizabeth's point of view — he never received favor, nor lands, nor gifts, nor title, nor hope for his children, nothing. He only earned a tomb by her side at Spilsby. Was he less a victim? Was Hugh Latimer, too, Catherine's friend and mentor, less a victim? He died in terrible agony, burning at the stake on a rainy day, when the fire wouldn't light. Horrible! These men and women were all victims to the enemies of their concepts and convictions. Not one was spared on account of his or her sex.

I AM pleading for the universality of these women's lives, transcending gender, or rather unifying the genders within what the German Protestant world calls *theologische Existenz*. These women existed theologically. They said it and we know it. Yet I still experience their stories as unbearably moving. Is it their fragility, their exposure to total loss and martyrdom? Is it their powerlessness in the face of inexorable powers? Is it the protectiveness of Burghley and of Bale and of Bertie, even the redemption of Henry Grey, male "father-figures" to these sterling women, which stirs in me something similar?

I come down on the side of Jane's words to Roger Ascham at Bradgate Park. So put upon and "nipped" and pressed upon by her whole external world that she turned to Plato, to the paradise of thought, to the Christlike compensation of her tutor Master Aylmer, to her "only pleasure": the consolation of (the Father in) theology. Jane had nothing with which to bargain. Everything was against her: her youth, her sex, her "protectors," her mother and her father, her despised Reformed Religion, her royal blood, her short stature. Yet her witness, her light, is incandescent.

All this is the crux of Christianity. Jane preeminently, with all these women who were the mothers of the English Reformation, partook of *theologische Existenz*. This means that they were part of the presence of God's absence, the unself-conscious reenactment of the *deus absconditus* of Matthew 27:46. If their gender's suscepti-bility to others' domination contributed to this, it is the universal human exposure to domination and destruction which their story tells. Jane Grey, Anne Boleyn, Katharine Parr, Anne Askew, Catherine Willoughby, even with their men: theirs was the pil-grim's progress of life beneath the shadow of the cross, the quin-tessence of human suffering interpreted by story.

Epilogue

Mary Zahl

The account of these mothers of the English Reformation is both moving and challenging. As I ponder this picture of their lives, I ask myself: What is it I admire in them? Am I personally indebted to them, and if so, how? What can I learn from them today?

WHAT DO I ADMIRE ABOUT
THESE FIVE WOMEN?

I admire their courage most of all. All of them risked their lives, and three of them lost theirs, because they stepped out in courage to defend the Gospel. They did not seek a cause; they were overtaken by it. There is much in common with the statement of Martin Luther, "Here I stand. I can do no other." These are not women trying to write their names into the history books. They are simply witnessing to what they believed to be true: the scales had fallen, the light had shone, and they would die rather than deny it.

In the same vein, I admire the fact that none of them succumbed to rationalization, to "justified" political shortcuts, or even to hiding behind their men. While it is true that Katharine Parr did a quickstep to convince Henry of her devotion to him, she did not deny her Lord or tell on her friends to save herself. She, and the other four, were convinced that being faithful was more important than life itself. I find that triumph of principle over self-interest especially rare and impressive in today's light.

While I naturally relate to them because they are women, I am struck by the differences between their world and mine, chiefly that I live in a time of opportunity for all women which they did not enjoy. What would they think of my career, which is separate from my husband's? What would they think of ordained women in the church? What would they think of the fact that most fine universities now have more female than male students? Would they not envy the way we decide whom to marry, essentially free from family machinations? Would they not envy our ability to support ourselves financially? These women strike me as exceptions, as there always have been exceptional women, who were able to work successfully in a system which worked against them. Did this struggle, in fact, help to *produce* their courage? Are our opportunities making us softer?

HOW AM I PERSONALLY INDEBTED TO THEM?

The most important idea which affects my own spiritual life is that they rightly set forth a doctrine of *unmediated access to God through Christ alone.* Were it not for them and their male counterparts, my church would still think it necessary to go through a representative of the church, i.e., *a male priest,* in order to approach God. The Reformers, including these five women, took seriously the veil of the temple's being torn open for all believers through the death of Christ. That meant direct access to Scripture, direct access through prayer, direct access to the fellowship of other believers. It is no accident that whenever the Gospel catches fire, as it did with Jesus, so in the early church, the Reformation, and even the beginning of Methodism, the doors are flung open for women. Only the institutionalization of the faith puts women down in the way which Christianity is often accused of doing.

Were it not for the Reformation which these women fought and died for, there would be no married clergy, and hence no clergy spouses. That would be a great loss. There would certainly be no ordained women, yet another loss to the church. And there is a further personal indebtedness which I and many other Americans share: because England became the haven for persecuted European Protestants, my own forbears fled there from Germany in the early eighteenth century, and were given land in South Carolina! Do I not have Katharine Parr and Elizabeth Tudor to thank?

WHAT CAN I LEARN FROM THEM TODAY?

Study the Bible. Try to see it through their eyes as the life-source that it was as they were able to read it for the first time.

Be courageous. There is nothing to fear if my status is secure in Christ and death has lost its sting. The consequences of exercising or not exercising courage can affect generations.

See God as my only authority. That is a wonderful and fearsome thing. It gives me enormous freedom, and tremendous responsibility.

Be grateful that I am not being asked to die for my faith, though I stand on the shoulders of many Christians who have. Pray for those who are being persecuted now.

Appendix A

Letter of Thomas Cranmer to Henry VIII, May 3, 1536 (Excerpt)

I am in such a perplexity, that my mind is clearly amazed; for I never had better opinion in woman, than I had in her; which maketh me to think, that she should not be culpable. And again, I think your Highness would not have gone so far, except she had surely been culpable. Now I think that your Grace best knoweth, that next unto your Grace I was most bound unto her of all creatures living. . . . And if she be found culpable, considering your Grace's goodness towards her, and what condition your Grace of your only mere goodness took her and set the Crown upon her head; I repute him not your Grace's faithful servant and subject, nor true unto the realm, that would not desire the offence without mercy to be punished to the example of all other. And as I loved her not a little for the love which I judged her to bear toward God and his gospel; so, if she be proved culpable, there is not one that loveth God and his gospel that ever will favour her, but must hate

---

As quoted in Diarmaid MacCulloch, *Thomas Cranmer* (New Haven: Yale University Press, 1996), p. 157.

her above all other; and the more they favour the gospel, the more they will hate her. . . .

And though she have offended so, that she hath deserved never to be reconciled unto your Grace's favour; yet almighty God hath manifoldly declared his goodness towards your Grace, and never offended you. . . . Wherefore I trust that your Grace will bear no less entire favour unto the truth of the gospel, than you did before; forsomuch as your Grace's favour to the gospel was not led by affection unto her, but by zeal unto the truth.

From the Examinations of Anne Askew, March 1545

He [Christopher Dare] asked me wherefore I said that I had rather read five lines in the Bible than to hear five masses in the temple. I confessed that I said no less: not for the dispraise of either the epistle or the gospel; but because the one did greatly edify me, and the other nothing at all. (p. 149)

Beside this, my Lord Mayor laid one thing unto my charge which was never spoken of me, but of them; and that was, whether a mouse eating the host received God, or no? This question did I never ask; but, indeed, they asked it of me, whereunto I made them no answer, but smiled. (154)

Then he asked me why I had so few words. And I answered, God hath given me the gift of knowledge, but not of utterance. And Solomon saith that "woman of few words is a gift of God." (Proverbs XIX) (170)

Then my lord chancellor [i.e., the Lord Wriothesley] asked me

---

All quotes from *Select Works of Bishop Bale*, edited for the Parker Society by the Rev. Henry Christmas (Cambridge: The University Press, 1849).

of my opinion in the Sacrament. My answer was this: I believe that so oft as I in a Christian congregation, do receive the bread, in remembrance of Christ's death, and with thanksgiving, according to his holy instruction, I receive therewith also the fruits of his most glorious passion. The bishop of Winchester [Stephen Gardner] bade me make a direct answer. I said, I would not sing a new song to the Lord in a strange land. (199)

Then came master Paget to me with many glorious words, and desired me to speak my mind to him. I might (he said) deny it again, if need were. I said that I would not deny the truth. He asked me how I could avoid the very words of Christ, "Take, eat; this is my body, which shall be broken for you." I answered, that Christ's meaning was there, as in (those) other places of the scripture: "I am the door" (John X.), "I am the vine" (John XV.), "Behold the Lamb of God" (John i.), "The rock-stone was Christ" (I Cor. X.), and such other like. You may not here, said I, take Christ for the material thing that he is signified by; for then ye will make him a very door, a vine, a lamb, and a stone, clean contrary to the Holy Ghost's meaning. All those, indeed, do signify Christ, like as the bread doth his body in that place. And though he did say there, "Take, eat this in remembrance of me;" yet did he not bid them hang up that bread in a box, and make it a God, or bow to it. (203)

THEN master Rich sent me to the Tower, where I remained till three of the clock. Then came Rich and one of the council, charging me, upon my obedience, to shew unto them if I knew man or woman of my sect. My answer was that I knew none. Then they asked me of my lady of Suffolk [i.e., Catherine Willoughby!], my lady of Sussex, my lady of Hertford, my lady Denny, and my lady Fitzwilliam. I said, that if I should pronounce any thing against them, I were not able to prove it. (220)

Then they did put me on the rack, because I confessed no ladies or gentlewomen to be of my opinion; and thereon they kept me a long time: and because I lay still, and did not cry, my lord chancellor and master Rich took pains to rack me in their own hands, till I was nigh dead. (224)

Then the lieutenant caused me to be loosed from the rack. Incontinently I swooned, and then they recovered me again. After that I sat two long hours recovering with my lord chancellor, upon the bare floor, where as he with many flattering words persuaded me to leave my opinion. But my Lord God (I thank his everlasting goodness) gave me grace to persevere, and will do (I hope) to the very end. (226)

Then was I brought to an house, and laid in a bed, with as weary and painful bones as ever had patient Job, I thank my Lord God thereof. Then my lord chancellor sent me word, if I would leave my opinion, I should want nothing: if I would not, I should forth to Newgate, and so be burnt. I sent him again word, that I would rather die than break my faith. Thus the Lord open the eyes of their blind hearts, that the truth may take place! Farewell, my dear friend, and pray, pray, pray. (227)

From *Lamentations of a Sinner* (1547), by Katharine Parr

Oh, how miserably and wretchedly am I confounded, when, for the multitude and greatness of my sins, I am compelled to accuse myself! Was it not a marvellous unkindness, when God did speak to me, and also call to me, that I would not answer him? What man, so called, would not have heard? Or what man, hearing, would not have answered? If an earthly prince had spoken, or called, I suppose there are none, but would willingly have done both. Now, therefore, what a wretch and caitiff am I, that, when the Prince of princes, the King of kings, did speak many pleasant and gentle words unto me, and also called me so many and sundry times, that they cannot be numbered; and yet, notwithstanding these great signs and tokens of love, I would not come unto him, but hid myself out of his sight, seeking many crooked and by-ways, wherein I walked so long, that I had wholly lost his sight. And no marvel, or wonder, for I had a blind guide, called Ignorance, who dimmed so mine eyes, that I could never perfectly get any sight of the fair, goodly, straight, and right ways of his doctrine; but continually travelled, uncomfortably, in foul, wicked, crooked, and perverse ways; yea, and because they were so much haunted of many, I could not think, but that I walked in the perfect and right way, having more regard to the number of the walkers, than to the order of the walking; believing also, most assuredly, with company, to have walked to heaven, whereas, I am most sure, they would have brought me down to hell.

I forsook the spiritual honouring of the true living God, and worshipped visible idols, and images made of men's hands, believing, by them, to have gotten heaven; yea, to say the truth, I made a great idol of myself, for I loved myself better than God. And, certainly, look, how many things are loved, or preferred, in our hearts, before God, so many are taken and esteemed for idols, and false gods. Alas! how have I violated this holy, pure, and most high precept and commandment of the love of God! Which precept bindeth me to love him with my whole heart, mind, force, strength, and understanding: and I, like unto an evil, wicked, and disobedient child, have given my will, power, and senses, to the contrary, making, almost, of every earthly and carnal thing, a god!

Furthermore, the blood of Christ was not reputed by me sufficient for to wash me from the filth of my sins; neither such ways, as he had appointed by his word; but I sought for such riffraff as the bishop of Rome hath planted in his tyranny and kingdom, trusting, with great confidence, by the virtue and holiness of them, to receive full remission of my sins. And so I did, as much as was in me, obfuscate and darken the great benefit of Christ's passion, than the which, no thought can conceive anything of more value. There cannot be done so great an injury and displeasure to almighty God, our Father, as to tread under foot Christ, his only begotten and well beloved Son. All other sins in the world, gathered together in one, are not so heinous and detestable in the sight of God. And no wonder, for, in Christ crucified, God doth show himself most noble and glorious, even an almighty God, and most loving Father, in his only dear and chosen blessed Son.

I THINK no less, but many will wonder and marvel at this my saying, that I never knew Christ for my Saviour and Redeemer until this time. For many have this opinion, saying, Who knoweth not there is a Christ? Who, being a christian, doth not confess him his Saviour? And thus believing their dead, human, historical faith and knowledge, which they have learned in their scholastical books to be the true infused faith and knowledge of Christ, which may be had, as I said before, with all sin, they used to say, by their own experience of themselves, that their faith doth not justify them. And true it is, except they have this faith, which I have declared here before, they shall never be justified.

And yet it is not false that by faith only I am sure to be justified. Even this is the cause that so many impugn this office and duty of true faith, because so many lack the true faith. And even as the faithful are forced to allow this true faith, so the unfaithful can, in nowise probably, entreat thereof; the one feeling in himself that which he saith, the other not having in him for to say.

I have certainly no curious learning to defend this matter withal, but a simple zeal and earnest love to the truth inspired of God, who promiseth to pour his Spirit upon all flesh; which I have, by the grace of God, whom I must humbly honour, felt in myself to be true.

Appendix D

The Examination of Lady Jane Grey, February 10, 1554

Feckenham. Madam, I lament your heavy case, and yet I doubt not but that you bear this sorrow of yours with a constant and patient mind.

Jane. You are welcome unto me, sir, if your coming be to give christian exhortation. And as for my heavy case, I thank God, I do so little lament it, that rather I account the same for a more manifest declaration of God's favour towards me, than ever he showed me at any time before. And therefore there is no cause why either you or others, who bear me good will, should lament or be grieved with my case, being a thing so profitable for my soul's health.

F. I am here come to you at this present, sent from the queen and her council, to instruct you in the true doctrine of the right faith, although I have so great confidence in you, that I have, I trust, little need to travail with you much therein.

From *The Renaissance in England*, edited by J. V. Cunningham (New York: Harcourt, Brace & World, 1966), pp. 14-18.

J. I heartily thank the queen's highness, who is not unmindful of her humble subject; and I hope likewise that you no less will do your duty therein, both truly and faithfully, according to that you were sent for.

F. What is then required of a christian?

J. That he should believe in God the Father, in God the Son, and in God the Holy Ghost, three persons one God.

F. Is there nothing else to be required or looked for in a christian, but to believe in him?

J. Yes; we must also love him with all our heart, with all our soul, and with all our mind, and our neighbour as ourself.

F. Why, then faith only justifies not, or saves not.

J. Yes, verily, faith, as Paul saith, only justifieth.

F. Why, St. Paul saith, If I have all faith, without love, it is nothing.

J. True it is; for how can I love him whom I trust not? or how can I trust him whom I love not? Faith and love go both together, and that love is comprehended in faith.

F. How shall we love our neighbour?

J. To love our neighbour is to feed the hungry, to clothe the naked, and give drink to the thirsty, and to do to him as we would be done to.

F. Why, then it is necessary unto salvation to do good works also; it is not sufficient only to believe.

J. I deny that, and I affirm that faith only saveth; but it is meet for a christian to do good works, in token that he follows the steps of his Master, Christ, yet may we not say that they profit to our salvation; for when we have done all, we are unprofitable servants, and faith only in Christ's blood saves us.

F. How many sacraments are there?

J. Two — the one, the sacrament of baptism; and the other, the sacrament of the Lord's supper.

F. No; there are seven.

J. By what scripture find you that?

F. Well, we will talk of that hereafter. But what is the signification of your two sacraments?

J. By the sacrament of baptism, I am washed with water, and regenerated by the Spirit. And that washing is a token to me that I am the child of God. The sacrament of the Lord's supper offered unto me, is a sure seal and testimony that I am by the blood of Christ, which he shed for me on the cross, made partaker of the everlasting kingdom.

F. Why, what do you receive in that sacrament? Do you not receive the very body and blood of Christ?

J. No, surely; I do not so believe. I think that at that supper I neither receive flesh nor blood, but only bread and wine, which bread, when it is broken, and the wine, when it is drunken, puts me in mind how that for my sins the body of Christ was broken, and his blood shed on the cross; and with that bread and wine I receive the benefits that come by the breaking of his body, and shedding of his blood on the cross for my sins.

F. Why, does not Christ speak these words, Take, eat, this is my body? Require you plainer words? does he not say it is his body?

J. I grant he saith so; and so he saith, I am the vine, I am the door; but he is never the more for that a door or a vine. Does not St. Paul say, He calleth those things that are not, as though they were? (Rom. iv) God forbid that I should say that I eat the very natural body and blood of Christ; for then either I should pluck away my redemption, or else there were two bodies or two Christs, or twelve bodies, when his disciples did eat his body, and it suffered not till the next day. So finally one body was tormented on the cross; and if they did eat another body, then had he two bodies; or, if his body were eaten, then it was not broken upon the cross. Or, if it were broken upon the cross, it was not eaten of his disciples.

F. Why, is it not as possible that Christ by his power could make his body both to be eaten and broken, as to be born of a virgin, as to walk upon the sea, having a body, and other such-like miracles as he wrought by his power only?

J. Yes, verily; if God would have done at his supper any miracle, he might have done so; but I say, that he minded to work no miracle, but only to break his body, and to shed his blood on the cross, for our sins. But I pray you answer me to this one question, Where was Christ when he said, Take, eat, this is my body? was he not at the table when he said so? he was at that time alive, and suffered not till the next day. What took he but bread? what brake he but bread? and what gave he but bread? Yea, what he took, that he brake; and look what he brake, he gave; yea, and what he gave, he did eat: and yet all this while he himself was alive, and at supper before his disciples, or else they were deceived.

F. You ground your faith upon such authors as say and unsay, both with a breath, and not upon the church, to whom you ought to give credit.

J. No, I ground my faith upon God's word, and not upon the church; for if the church be a good church, the faith of the church must be tried by God's word, and not God's word by the church, nor yet my faith. Shall I believe the church because of antiquity, or shall I give credit to the church that takes away from me the one half of the Lord's supper, and will suffer no layman to receive it in both kinds? But surely I think if they deny it to us, then deny they to us part of our salvation. And I say, that it is an evil church, and not the spouse of Christ, but the spouse of the devil, that alters the Lord's supper, and both takes from it, and adds to it. To that church, say I, God will add plagues, and from that church will he take their part out of the book of life. Do they learn that of St. Paul, when he ministered to the Corinthians in both kinds? Shall I believe this church? God forbid!

F. That was done for a good intent of the church, to avoid a heresy that sprung upon it.

J. Why, shall the church alter God's will and ordinance for good intent? How did king Saul? The Lord God forbid.

To this M. Feckenham gave me a long, tedious, yet eloquent reply, using many strong and logical persuasions to compel me to lean to their church; but my faith had armed my resolution to withstand any assault that words could then use against me. Of many other articles of religion we reasoned, but these formerly rehearsed were the chief, and most effectual.

Jane Dudley.

After this, Feckenham took his leave, saying, that he was sorry for her; for I am sure, quoth he, that we two shall never meet.

True it is, said the lady Jane, that we shall never meet, except God turn your heart; for I am assured, unless you repent, and turn to God, you are in an evil case; and I pray God, in the bowels of his mercy, to send you his Holy Spirit, for he hath given you his great gift of utterance, if it pleased him also to open the eyes of your heart.

Two Letters of Catherine Willoughby

To William and Mildred Cecil, March 4, 1559
(Concerning the Reformation of the church)

The hand within the letter seemeth to be my Lady your wife's, the superscription Sir William Cecil's; but howsoever it be it is all one, yea, and so I would to God all our whole nation were likewise one in Jesus Christ as behooveth. Nay, if there be but eleven about her Majesty's person that savor one thing in Him she is happy and the whole realm. But alack, the report is otherwise, which is an intolerable heaviness to such as love God and her; yea, and that such as should rather be spurred holdeth her Majesty of her own good inclination, running most back, among which you are specially named. Wherefore, for the love I bear you I cannot forbear to write it; and if it shall please you to heed a simple woman's mind.

From Evelyn Read, *My Lady Suffolk: A Portrait of Catherine Willoughby, Duchess of Suffolk* (New York: Alfred Knopf, 1964).

Undoubtedly the greatest wisdom is not to be too wise, which, of all others, you should by experience chieflyest know. For if there were anything whereby that good duke, your old master, deserved and felt the heavy stroke of God, what is there else whereof men may accuse him but only that when God had placed him to set forth His glory (which yet of himself he was always ready to do) but being still plucked by the sleeve of [by] worldly friends, for this worldly respect or that, in fine gave over his hot zeal to set forth God's true religion as he had most nobly begun, and turning him to follow such worldly devices, you can as well as I tell what came of it: the duke lost all that he sought to keep, with his head to boot, and his counsellors slipped their collars, turned their coats and hath served since to play their parts in many other matters. But [to] beware in time is good, for though God wink at them He sleepeth not and will undoubtedly at length pay such turncoats home. Wherefore I am forced to say with the prophet Elie, how long halt ye between two opinions? . . .

If the Mass be good, tarry not to follow it nor take from it no part of that honour which the last queen, with her notable stoutness, brought it to and left in (wherein she deserved immortal praise seeing she was so persuaded that it was good) but if you be not so persuaded, alas, who should move the Queen's Majesty to honour it with her presence, or any of her counsellors? Well, it is so reported here that her Majesty tarried but the Gospel and so departed. I pray God that no part of that report were true, for in conscience there is few of you that can excuse yourselves but that you know there is no part of it good after that sort as they use it; for the very Gospel there read is unprofitable or rather an occasion of falling to the multitude which, hearing it and not understanding it, taketh it rather for some holy charm than any other thing. Saints' faces may in Lent be covered (and it were good they were always so) but where Christ is He is bare faced, and specially where He hath openly preached at noon days. . . . To build surely is first to lay the sure cornerstone, today and not tomorrow; there is no exception by man's law that may serve against God's.

There is no fear of innovation in restoring old good laws and repealing new evil, but it is to be feared men have so long worn the Gospel slopewise that they will not gladly have it again straight to their legs. Christ's plain coat without a seam is fairer to the older eyes than all the jaggs of Germany; this I say for that it is also said here that certain Dutchers [i.e., Germans] should commend to us the confession of Augsberg [sic] as they did to the Poles, where it was answered by a wise counsellor [that] neither Augsberg neither Rome were their ruler but Christ, who hath left His Gospel behind Him a rule sufficient and only to be followed.

To William Cecil, Easter Monday 1580
(Concerning her daughter-in-law Mary Vere)

I am ashamed to be so troublesome to your Lordship and others of my good Lords of her Majesty's honourable council, specially in so uncomfortable a suit as for license of their assent of the absence of my only dear son, in whose company I hoped with comfort to have finished my last days. But . . . either I must see his doleful pining and vexed mind at home, which hath brought him to such a state of mind and body as so many knoweth and can witness it, or else content myself with his desire to seek such fortune abroad as may make him forget some griefs and give him better knowledge and experience to serve her Majesty and his country at his return. The time he desireth for the same is five years, so as I am never like after his departure to see him again; yet am I loath he should so long be out of her Majesty's realm wherefore I cannot consent to any more than three years.

Oh, my good Lord, you have children and therefore you know how dear they be to their parents, your wisdom also is some help to govern your fatherly affections by . . . but alas, I a poor woman which with great pains and travail many years hath by God's mercy brought an only son from tender youth to man's state . . . so hoping now to have reaped some comfort for my long pains . . . in place of comfort I myself must be the suitor for his absence, to my great grief and sorrow. But God's will be fulfilled, who worketh all for the best to them that love and fear Him; *wherefore were not that hope of Him thoroughly settled in me, I think my very heart would burst for sorrow* [ital. PZ]. I understand my sharp letters be everywhere showed, but were the bitter causes that moved them as well opened and known, I am sure my very enemies . . . would not only pity me and my husband's wrongs but both my children's. . . . I most humbly beseech her Majesty even for God's sake therefore to give him leave to go to sea and live in all places where it shall please God to hold him, always with the duty of a faithful subject to serve . . . her Majesty.

Select Family Tree

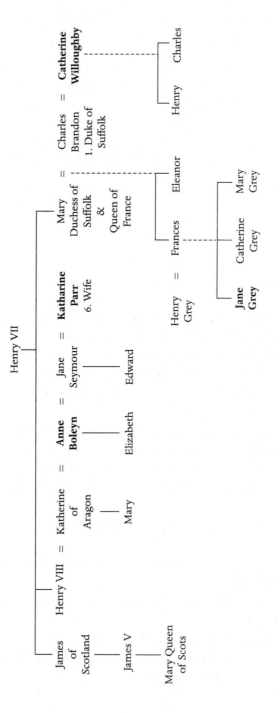

Anne Askew was not of royal blood.

Reading List

Ascham, Roger. *The Schoolmaster* (1570). Edited by Laurence V. Ryan. Charlottesville: University Press of Virginia, 1967.

Bale, John. *Select Works of Bishop Bale.* Edited for The Parker Society by the Rev. Henry Christmas. Cambridge: The University Press, 1849.

Beilin, Elaine V., ed. *The Examinations of Anne Askew.* New York: Oxford University Press, 1996.

Bradstreet, Anne. *Anne Bradstreet: Selections from Her Works.* Compiled by Nancy V. Weare. Ipswich and North Andover: Friends of the Ipswich Public Library and the Stevens Memorial Library, 1998.

Chapman, Hester W. *Lady Jane Grey: The Setting of the Reign.* London: Jonathan Cape, 1962.

————. *The Last Tudor King: A Study of Edward VI.* London: Jonathan Cape, 1961.

D'Aubigné, Agrippa. *Les Tragiques.* Edited by Jacques Bailbé. Paris: Flammarian, 1968.

Dickens, A. G. *The English Reformation.* 2nd edition. London: B. T. Batsford, 1989.

Hannay, Margaret Patterson, ed. *Silent But for the Word: Tudor Women as Patrons, Translations, and Writers of Religious Works.* Kent, OH: Kent State University Press, 1985.

The Heptameron: Tales and Novels of Marguerite Queen of Navarre. Translated by W. K. Kelly. London: Privately printed, no date.

Ives, E. W. *Anne Boleyn.* Oxford: Basil Blackwell, 1986.

James, Susan E. *Katheryn Parr: The Making of a Queen.* Ashgate: Aldershut, 1999.

MacCulloch, Diarmaid. *Thomas Cranmer.* New Haven: Yale University Press, 1996.

————. *Tudor Church Militant: Edward VI and the Protestant Reformation.* London: Penguin, 1999.

Marot, Clément. *Oeuvres Complètes de Clément Marot.* 2 vols. Edited by B. Saint-Marc. Paris: Garnier Frères, 1879.

Matthew, David. *Lady Jane Grey: The Setting of the Reign.* London: Eyre Methuen, 1972.

Read, Evelyn. *My Lady Suffolk: A Portrait of Catherine Willoughby, Duchess of Suffolk.* New York: Alfred Knopf, 1964.

Roelker, Nancy Lyman. *Queen of Navarre: Jeanne d'Albret.* Cambridge: Harvard University Press, 1968.

Smith, A. C. H. *Lady Jane:* A novel from the screenplay by David Edgar. New York: Holt, Rinehart and Winston, 1985.

The Writings of Edward VI, Katharine Parr, Anne Askew, Lady Jane Grey, Hamilton and Balnaves. British Reformers, vol. 3. London: The Religious Tract Society, 1830.

The Writings of John Fox, Bale, and Coverdale. British Reformers, vol. 12. London: The Religious Tract Society, 1830.

Zeller, Reimar. *Prediger des Evangeliums. Erben der Reformation im Spiegel der Kunst.* Regensburg: Schnell and Steiner, 1998.